A Fly-Fishing Newbie

(The First Three Years)

Dave Cartier

© 2007 Dave Cartier
All Rights Reserved

ISBN: 978-1-4303-1753-1

Dedication

I dedicate this book to my wife Nancy. She has always given me her unwavering support, encouragement and advice in whatever I have attempted to do. As I have said numerous times, I may have failed in many things that I have tried in my life, but I became a success when she consented to be my wife.

Acknowledgements

I would like to thank the many people who have helped me to learn and enjoy the sport of fly-fishing (so far). Because I am an engineer and love to learn, I am like a sponge around people more knowledgeable than I am about something. One of the great things about fly-fishing is that everyone wants to help you. All I had to do was ask, and someone would give me advice, point me to a great fishing spot or anything else that I needed at the time. Thank you all.

Thanks also go out to the gang at the Northern Virginia Chapter of Trout Unlimited. I especially encourage the reader to join an organization like TU. It's a great way to learn about fly-fishing through their speakers at the monthly meetings, or by going on their "Fish with a Member" trips. In addition, they are working to protect fish habitat throughout the United States and the World, which is not only good for the fish's environment, but also, for the environment in general.

Lastly, I would like to express my gratitude to Harry Murray, Jeff Murray, Newell Steele and Tom Brtalik for allowing me to use some of the material that I received from them in the courses, chats and lectures that they gave while I was writing this book.

Photo Credits

Many of the photos in this book were taken by my wife, Nancy Cartier.

Table of Contents

1 Introduction 1
2 Why I Took Up Fly-fishing 4
3 The First Purchase 5
4 Early Fishing 6
5 The Two Day Introductory School 9
6 Joining Trout Unlimited 16
7 Getting My Waders and Boots 18
8 Catching Fish in Spite of Myself 20
   8.1 My First Brookie 22
   8.2 My First Smallie (on a fly) 25
9 Mountain Trout Saturday Class and School 28
   9.1 Mountain Trout Saturday Class 28
   9.2 Mountain Trout School 31
10 Shad Fiasco and Redemption 40
11 Nymphing 47
12 Tying Flies 51
13 Odds and Ends 55
   13.1 Thoughts on Leaders 55
   13.2 Knots and Loops for Rigging 57
   13.3 The 16-20 Knot 60
   13.4 The Uni-knot (Duncan Loop) 63
   13.5 Casting 66
   13.6 Fishing Trip List 68
   13.7 Trout Stuff 71
14 References 73
15 Appendix A Places to Fish and Some Fish Stories 74
   15.1 Mainly Sunfish 74
   15.2 Mainly Stocked Rainbow Trout 75
   15.3 Mainly Brook Trout 76
   15.4 Mainly Smallmouth Bass (near Washington, D. C.) 80
   15.5 Mainly Smallmouth Bass (Front Royal, Woodstock, etc.) 81
   15.6 Mainly Smallmouth Bass (Near Culpeper, VA) 83
16 Appendix B My Flybox Contents 86
17 Appendix C ROSS Cimarron 3 Reel Setup 89
18 Appendix D After-Season Fishing Gear Cleanup 90
19 Appendix E Tam and I 92
20 Index 94

Table of Figures

Figure 1-1 Kid's Day at Bon Air Park 2
Figure 4-1 A Manassas Battlefield Pond 6
Figure 4-2 Original Vest (Left) and High Riding Fishing Vest (Right) 8
Figure 8-1 Shenandoah Mountain Brook Trout 24
Figure 9-1 A Pool in the Blue Ridge Mountains at Trout School 31
Figure 9-2 A 12 Inch Brook Trout 37
Figure 10-1 Sinking Tip Leader Loop 42
Figure 10-2 My First Shad 44
Figure 10-3 My First Perch (on a fly) 44
Figure 11-1 Gold Ribbed Bead Head Hare's Ear Nymph 48
Figure 12-1 L. L. Bean Fly-tying Starter Kit 51
Figure 12-2 My Cheapo Vise 52
Figure 12-3 My Hare's Ear Nymph 54
Figure 13-1 Knotted Leader Section with Strike Indicator 56
Figure 13-2 Forming the 16-20 Knot (Part 1) 62
Figure 13-3 Forming the 16-20 Knot (Part 2) 62
Figure 13-4 Forming the 16-20 Knot (Part 3) 63
Figure 13-5 Forming the Uni-knot Loop (Part 1) 64
Figure 13-6 Forming the Uni-knot Loop (Part 2) 65
Figure 13-7 Forming the Uni-knot Loop (Part 3) 65
Figure 16-1 Trout Flybox Contents 87
Figure 16-2 Bass/Shad Flybox Contents 88
Figure 19-1 My Dog Tam 92

List of Tables

Table 5-1 L. L. Bean Two Day Fly-fishing School Notes 9
Table 6-1 Trout Unlimited Activities 16
Table 9-1 Mountain Trout Fishing School Notes April 11, 2005 33
Table 10-1 Sinking Tips and Sinking Lines 41
Table 11-1 Top Water versus Nymphing Observations 49
Table 13-1 Knotted versus Unknotted Leaders Pros and Cons 57
Table 13-2 Rod/Reel Connections 58
Table 13-3 Dave's Fishing Checklist 68
Table 15-1 Strasburg River Gauge Reading Relative to Wade-ability 82
Table 17-1 ROSS Cimarron 3 Specifications 89

1 Introduction

One day in 2006, while driving to a Trout Unlimited stream cleanup event in preparation for a Teens' and Kids' Fishing Day (see the picture below), I thought that if ever I were going to write about my learning experience with fly-fishing, it should be now while I am making the transition from "Newbie" to "Somewhat Proficient." I have come from knowing absolutely nothing about fly-fishing to being reasonably good at it. At least I can catch fish consistently and, more importantly, most of the time I know why I am catching them.

I took up fly-fishing immediately after retirement primarily as a way of getting myself out of the house. I do a lot of things on the computer and so I could have conceivably spent most of my time indoors. This, I knew, was not good for me. Fly-fishing (actually any fishing technique) is a wonderful way to connect with nature and get away from the din of modern life. I am sure glad that I have discovered this wonderful activity. A story will illustrate what I mean.

While cleaning up "Four Mile Run" (a Northern Virginia steam) at Bon Air Park one day (along with other Trout Unlimited volunteers led by John Hadley), I was standing in the stream with my trash bag when a family with two boys came along. They were cleaning up the banks. I told one of the boys that I was having more fun than he was because I was in the stream and he was on the bank. I said that when you are a boy (or girl) you can do a lot of things and no one says "You're too grown up to do that!" At some age people think that you have to be a grownup and leave your childhood behind.

Fly-fishing allows me to be a kid again, standing in streams, climbing over rocks, and even turning a few of them over to find out what is in the stream that will help me catch fish. Fly-fishing also gives me the opportunity to go to some of the most beautiful places in the world right here in my Northern Virginia backyard.

Figure 1-1 Kid's Day at Bon Air Park

Okay, that is why I started fly-fishing, but why this book? Since there are a myriad of books written by expert fly-fishing men and women, I could not possibly add anything new to the knowledge base that they provide. However, as an electrical engineer, I tend to want to know why things are the way they are. I am an extremely logical person (Mr. Spock on Star Trek is my idea of a normal person), and I have written down pretty much everything that I have learned over these last few years. So I thought that I could provide others who are new to fly-fishing, or who are contemplating taking up the sport, with some aspects of it that are uniquely associated with the process that takes place when one is just learning.

As a sort of disclaimer, however, I have to tell the reader up front that the statements made in this book, except where noted, are my own, based on my very few years of experience up to this point in time, plus my own innate logic. There are plenty of opinions and advice from others with much more expertise than I have on the subjects that I will discuss in the book, but I hope that my "newbie" perspective can show the reader that you don't have to get it perfect to have a lot of fun fly-fishing.

This book, my first, will be very focused. First of all since I live in Vienna, Virginia, almost all of my experience is with this area and the nearby Shenandoah Mountain streams and rivers. I do feel, however, that persons who live in other areas will also benefit from the book.

1 INTRODUCTION

The book will tell you how and why I chose the fishing gear that I have, some idea of cost (in the 2004/2005 time frame), how I fish (my techniques, albeit crude by expert standards), where I fish, etc. Most of the book comes from the journal that I have kept of my outings, talks at Trout Unlimited meetings, chats with fly shop proprietors, etc. The journal especially notes some things that I learned on a particular outing, all of which have brought me to my current level of expertise.

The main lesson that should be taken from this book is that **anyone can learn to fly-fish** and catch a lot of fish this way. You don't have to be a great caster, know how to match the hatch, or master other aspects of the sport before you can enjoy fly-fishing. Do what I did, get into fly-fishing, and learn what you need to know along the way. You will only get better and have more knowledge as time passes.

Finally, do **NOT** become overwhelmed with all of the fly patterns, hatches, etc. that are part of the sport. While knowing these things will **INCREASE** the number of fish that you catch, and allow you to present your fly in different ways, it is **NOT** needed to catch enough fish to make your outing worthwhile. As you grow in the sport you will naturally learn more and more. You can't help it! If you want to become an entomologist, you can; if you don't want to tie flies, you don't have to. You can simply go down to your favorite spot and throw your line in the water and enjoy not being at the office or stuck in traffic.

2 Why I Took Up Fly-fishing

I have told you that I took up fishing mainly to get myself out of the house after retirement, but why fly-fishing? About 20 years ago I was a spincast fisherman. I owned three rods and the usual tackle box filled with every lure under the sun that was guaranteed to catch fish. I had spinners, spoons, sluggos, worms, etc. I had my successes and failures and had a lot of fun.

The biggest problem for me, however, was that most of the time I needed a boat! I am sure that it would have been different if I had close access to a fishing pier or something like that, but I didn't. I didn't have a boat of my own, so I usually rented one. This meant that I needed to lug around a battery and an electric motor along with my tackle box, rods, fish finder and other accessories. I rented a boat for various reasons, chief among which was not wanting to deal with a trailer.

Don't get me wrong, I had lots of fun once on the water (usually a lake). A few times I took my wife and kids and we really enjoyed ourselves. However, I gave it up, and the main reason was the boat. When I could no longer rent one at a park on the Potomac River that was close to our house, I had to make a decision to either buy a boat or stop fishing. I chose the latter.

So why did I start fishing again and take up fly-fishing? I had seen movies and magazines of fly-fishing for quite some time, but thought of it as something above my skill level. This, as you will see later, is **ridiculous**! Anyone can learn to catch fish this way.

Anyway, a few years ago I was ready to retire from my job as a signal processing engineer with a Government support company. As many people do when confronted with this event, I needed to find ways to occupy all of the free time that I would now have. This prompted me to take a one hour introductory fly casting lesson ($12) from a very nice young man who worked for L. L. Bean in Tyson's Corner, Virginia.

To my surprise, I was able to cast (not well, but I could get the line in the general direction that I was aiming at). I came back ready to buy a rod and whatever else I needed to get started. It turned out that there was no one at the fly-fishing department to help me, so I went to the Orvis store down the street. By the way, I took my first fly-fishing class from L. L. Bean and have since dealt with a lot of really nice and knowledgeable persons at L. L. Bean as I will relate later in the book. It was just the luck of the draw that whoever was supposed to be at the desk was out to lunch or helping others in another department or otherwise engaged.

3 The First Purchase

So I was now at the Orvis store. I was helped by one of the salesmen who was pretty savvy on fly-fishing, at least relative to my expertise at the moment, which, come to think of it, was zero. I ended up with one of their introductory rods (a 5 weight), a reel that matched the rod, fly line, some tippet and flies.

Since this book is about my learning process, I will tell you that I have since added two other rod/reel outfits (one lighter - a 3 weight, and one heavier - a 7 weight) that better serve me for what I want to do in fly-fishing (more about that later). However, the 5 weight outfit that they put me into has caught a lot of fish, and has also saved a fishing trip from being a disaster when I forgot my 3 weight rod one time.

By the way, a lesson learned from forgetting the rod that I wanted to use is that you should really have a spare outfit that you always carry with you. So as soon as you get some idea of what you are doing and what you need, get another outfit. You will see what I mean if a rod breaks while fishing or you forget the outfit that you intended to use. You don't want to drive for a couple of hours and have the day totally ruined. By using my 5 weight, which was heavier than I would have liked, I made do and caught a good number of fish.

Now getting back to my first purchase, the salesman put me into a

- Clearwater Classic Midflex (their term for medium action) 7.5 foot 5 weight rod
- Clearwater Classic III reel
- 5 weight Fly line, Fly line Backing, 5x Leader and Tippet.

This cost me about $252.

Along with the above, I bought a DeLORME topographic map of Virginia (I highly recommend this) and four flies. The salesman also recommended a knot tying tool. It works, but I have since abandoned it because I don't want to get dependent on a tool if I can tie the knots without it. I would say that if you do use one, practice your knots without it from time-to-time for those occasions when you lose the tool or leave it in the car.

Now that I had my rod, reel, line, etc., I was all set to go fishing at a place that did not require waders and boots.

4 Early Fishing

When I first got into fishing many years ago, I went to a local sports store and talked to a very nice man who set me up with a ZEBCO spinning rod outfit, some line, hooks, sinkers and bobbers. He told me to get some worms, go to the lake and fish from the shore for bluegills (small sunfish). As we all know, if it weren't for bluegills, an awful lot of people would not be fishing today. These little guys make any fisherman (or woman) look good. They are large in number, always hungry, hard to spook, put up a nice fight and are not picky about what you offer to them.

Well, now I was getting into fly-fishing, right? Since I didn't have a clue about what I was doing, I decided to go to the Manassas Battlefield and try one of their ponds, one of which is shown in the picture below.

Figure 4-1 A Manassas Battlefield Pond

As usual the bluegills made my day. I threw a fly at them and they took it. Hey, this was fun! I was hooked! (Pardon the pun). I guess I can fly-fish. Let's forget that my cast landed nowhere near where I meant for it to go, and that it splashed on the water loud enough to scare away any self-respecting trout. The "Duty Bluegill" didn't care.

Even though I really enjoy my Shenandoah fishing spots with brook and rainbow trout, as well as the smallmouth bass and fall fish, I have gone back to the ponds many times. This was especially true in my early days wherever I got skunked in the mountain streams, needed some practice casting, or just wanted to have some fun without driving over an hour and a half.

Because one of my original reasons for getting into fly-fishing was to avoid dealing with a boat, I have not done any large lake fishing (except once from the shore of Lake Fairfax where I didn't catch anything). Some day I may get a float tube or pontoon boat and try it, but for now I like standing in a stream or river too much to consider it. [Since originally writing the previous paragraph, I have purchased a pontoon boat. I won't discuss this because I feel that it is beyond the "newbie" theme of this book. Let me just say that there is no motor or trailer needed and I can easily handle it all by myself.]

As a result of my initial fly-fishing experience at the ponds, I would like to give you tips that may help you in your journey. First of all, I started off with a fanny pack (a pouch that straps around the waist like a lot of people wear when traveling). An experienced fly-fisherwoman at L. L. Bean said that she liked to travel light and so used a fanny pack, and not a vest. This seemed logical to me.

I had a fanny pack that we took on vacations for our passports, cameras and such, so I naturally tried it first. When that wasn't big enough, I bought a "fly-fishing pack," that is, one made to carry all of your floatants, flies, etc. That one wasn't big enough either, so I bought a bigger one.

The bigger pack did the job, but I didn't like the limited space. Someone at Orvis suggested that I use the fanny pack, but put the extra stuff that I needed in a backpack. He said he carried his waders and boots in the backpack and that made the walking a lot easier. I tried it, but it had a major problem, at least for me. I had to keep picking up my backpack when I moved to a different pool. I suppose I could have planted it somewhere and picked it up on the way back, but I would then have to find it, plus "what if I didn't come back that way?"

So the fanny pack wouldn't serve my purposes for most fishing trips. By the way, it is not totally wasted since I now use it for fishing a stream near my house that I can walk to. It's nice not to have to carry the weight of the vest for the things that I will never use.

Having decided to use a vest, I bought one from Orvis. It was a lightweight vest (see the picture below) and carried all of my gear. I used it for about a year. The problem with it and any vest that extends near your hips is that whatever is in the lower pockets will get wet when you fall down (and you <u>will</u> fall down). You can get around this with Ziploc bags and such, but I didn't like it.

I happened to be watching a video tape on trout fishing one time and noticed that the author's vest rode high on his body. There were also two large pockets up by the shoulders and the other ones were higher up as well. I started looking for something like that. I looked in L. L. Bean, The Angler's Lie (a local flyshop that I will talk about later), Bass Pro and several catalogs. I finally went to the Orvis store. They showed me several Orvis brand vests, but none of them filled the bill. The salesman then showed me the Simms G3 Guide vest ($170) and I bought it. The figure below shows me with it on. Notice where the bottom of the vest is. For comparison, the figure also shows me with the vest that I had before this one. Again, notice where the bottom is and where the main pockets are. I put my wallet, keys and sandwich in one of the upper pockets to minimize their chances of getting wet if I fall.

Using a vest instead of a fanny pack, and the choice of a vest style itself, is a personal choice. I have given you the reasons for my choice; I hope that it helps so that you don't have to buy two fanny packs and a vest before finding the one that is perfect for you.

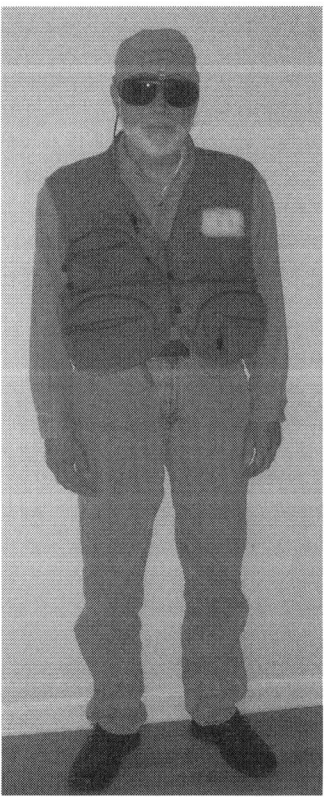 

Figure 4-2 Original Vest (Left) and High Riding Fishing Vest (Right)

5 The Two Day Introductory School

If you have a lot of time to learn fly-fishing you don't need to go to a school (just join a fly-fishing group like Trout Unlimited, be observant and ask questions). At my age, however, I needed to get up to a reasonable level of expertise pretty rapidly. So I signed up for the L. L. Bean two day introductory fly-fishing school in October 2003. It cost me $325 (plus the motel stay and food costs). It is part of their "Outdoor Discovery Schools" offerings. I chose this one because it was being held in Front Royal, Virginia. There are other schools and even guides that can get you up to speed, but I ended up with the Bean school and was very pleased.

The instructors for the school were really great. They were all very friendly, well-informed, and taught us a lot of facts and techniques.

The main thing that they concentrated on was casting, as you might expect. We casted a lot! They all watched us (even video taped us on one occasion) and analyzed our casts. By the end of the school all of us had decent casts. Since I don't practice my casting too much outside of fishing, I have lost the level of casting proficiency that I obtained at the school, but I still get the job done.

Besides casting, we did lots of other things over the two days, which included learning to recognize some bugs, trying different weight rods, learning some basics about fly-fishing like tackle, hooks, etc., and tying Wooly Buggers. I caught the first fish (a largemouth bass, albeit a small one) on the class fishing outing at their pond using my Wooly.

Here are some notes that I took during the two day school. It is interesting to review them at this stage of my experience to see what was important to me at the time, and to understand how much I have learned. I was overwhelmed with information in the beginning, but now some of it is just second nature to me. **Remember this!!!** Don't worry about not remembering everything that is presented to you. You will hear it again and again. Eventually, you will not have to memorize it; you will just "know" it.

Table 5-1   L. L. Bean Two Day Fly-fishing School Notes

I will state my original notes from the school with the "School" heading and, if I feel that I can add anything to what they told me at the school, I will give you my take on the subject based on my experience with the heading "Dave".

- **School:** For waders, Gortex is too bulky, whereas Neoprene is too hot. High waist waders are good. Separate boots are best, rather than boots integrated into the waders themselves.

  Dave: I ended up with a set of Orvis Pro Guide 2 Gortex chest waders with stocking feet. I then use lightweight wading boots over the wader stocking feet.

By the way, I may sound like a shill for Orvis, but since that is where I ended up on this particular item, I have to state it the way it is. I have since been told that Simms blows away Orvis waders. I can't say one way or the other since I haven't had a chance to try the Simms waders. All I can say is that I am very satisfied with my waders. They are comfortable and have held up well while climbing over rocks on the North Fork of the Shenandoah River and the Shenandoah Mountain streams, as well as going through briar patches in the woods. I recently tested them for leaks and they passed perfectly.

Some things that I have learned about waders are as follows:

- For a first purchase choose chest waders that can fold down to convert them into waist waders. I have never been too hot with my waders and can walk a long distance comfortably.

- I recommend stocking feet and separate boots. The separate boots give your feet better support and are more comfortable for walking and climbing.

- I bought felt soles with studs on my wading boots originally. They worked well, but I had to be very careful not to scratch any surfaces like floors and such. It was also more <u>uncomfortable</u> walking on rocky ground and/or pavement. I used them for 2 years and have since replaced them with just plain felt. We shall see if I slip a lot. [Since writing this I have gone fishing without the studs many times in Shenandoah Mountains streams and the Rappahannock River. I think that I slip a little more, but not much.]

By the way, it was very easy to tell when the felt soles needed replacement. They simply fall off the bottom of the boot leaving you with the rubber sole that they were attached to (so it doesn't ruin your outing; it just makes your footing slicker). I came home after a trip and found that both of my boots were missing the large part of the felt/stud sole. The smaller part on the heels was still there. I replaced everything, however, since they did not look like they had much wear left in them.

- From what I have seen, rubber soles even with a rough surface will result in slipping on any slime that you step on. I will stick with felt. Another plus is that they are easy to replace.

- o <u>Always wear a wading belt</u>. It can save your life! I fell into the North Fork of the Shenandoah River one time and it prevented my waders from filling up, not to mention keeping my legs dry.

- **School:** Use a wading stick

   Dave: I agree wholeheartedly!!! I have been saved several times from going in over my head in the river, and it makes walking in a stream or even in the woods much safer. I use it ahead of me to sweep my path for snakes and spider webs.

There are two main kinds of sticks. I use an inexpensive (about $30) expandable walking stick from L. L. Bean. I attach it to my wading belt with a small bungee cord. Sometimes I will wear it over my shoulder if I need to walk a long way on an open trail. Note that any stick will get caught on rocks and such, so the bungee cord is great as it lets me know with a tug on my belt without pulling me over.

There is another kind of wading stick that automatically expands and locks itself in place when you pull it out of its holster. It costs about $100 to $150 and folds up into the holster when you are not using it. It is very nice, but I didn't want to part with that much money considering that the one that I had did the job very well. I suppose that if I only used my wading stick occasionally while fishing, the folding up and being out of the way would be nice. However, I pretty much use my stick all the time, so this is not a great advantage to me, given the cost difference.

- **School:** When casting, pick up about 30 feet of line **at most**. More will be hard to pick up and do a good cast. Also, if there is not enough line out, then it will be hard to get the line to leave the rod on the cast.

   Dave: I have found this to be very true.

- **School:** Dry flies have bristly parts that hold air so they float.

   Dave: Obviously this is true. I might add that if the fly gets too wet, then dry it on your shirt and put floatant on it. Try to avoid turbulent water since this will usually sink a dry fly. See my chapter on Nymphing for more discussion on this subject.

- **School:** Streamers imitate fish, especially minnows.

   Dave: This is all that I wrote down, but I am sure that they mentioned that streamers also imitate leeches, crayfish and other things good to eat. We tied two Wooly Buggers at the school. From what I have read they are the most popular and effective streamer. I can personally vouch for their effectiveness on rainbow trout, bass, fall fish and, of course, bluegills.

- **School:** You can use a barbed hook for bony mouth fish. Barbs are harder to deal with, but result in more fish caught for beginners who don't know how to play the fish.

  Dave: From the beginning I have always mashed down the barbs. I have found that it is easier to get the hook out of the fish, doesn't tear it up so much, and is safer if I get stuck with one (I haven't so far, but I know that it will happen some day).

Since I have not lost a lot of fish using barb-less hooks, I would say that it doesn't affect the number of fish that you catch that much, and isn't worth putting up with the problems that barbs present. As for bony mouth fish, I can't say since I haven't caught any. It would seem logical, however.

- **School:** Choose the fish you want to catch and then match it to the weight of the fly line and then match it to the rod.

  Dave: For example, if all you want to go for are bluegills and small brook trout, then a 3 weight rod is all you really need. However, you will have a lot of trouble casting a heavy streamer with that rod.

Now is about as good a time as any to tell you what rods I have. As I said earlier in the book, my original rod and reel was a Clearwater Classic 5 weight outfit. These days I only use it as a backup, although it is a perfectly fine rod for a lot of fishing situations.

About a year later, I bought a 6 foot 10 inch 3 weight Scott rod with a Hardy Featherweight reel from Harry Murray in Edinburg, Virginia. I use this for the mountain trout where the overhead causes me a lot of trouble with the longer rod. I would get entangled in the trees that hang over the streams up in the mountains. I have found that with the shorter rod, I don't get as hung up as I used to. As to its action and weight, it is a joy to cast and so lightweight that you hardly know you have it in your hand. Oh, and it makes bluegills seem like tarpons.

Later in the season when the smallmouth bass are active, I like to go to the Rappahannock River near Culpeper or the Shenandoah River near Front Royal or Woodstock, Virginia. The 3 weight or the 5 weight will not throw the leadeyed hellgrammite that I have had so much success with. The fly is just too heavy. For this type of fishing I use a Sage 9 foot, 7 weight rod with a ROSS Cimarron 3 reel. It is a great rod, and the reel is the best of all 3 that I have. I say this because there is no (I mean NO) drag when you reel in the fish. Of course, you can set whatever drag that you want for playing the fish.

5 THE TWO DAY INTRODUCTORY SCHOOL

I purchased the 7 weight rod at The Angler's Lie in Arlington, Virginia on March 4, 2005; Dave "Grizzly" Lambert sold me the outfit. I told him about my bass fishing, but also that I wanted to try my hand at shad fishing when they come up the Potomac to spawn in the spring. This rod and reel is the perfect combination. I have caught many shad, smallies, fallfish, and bluegill on this rod. I love it.

Based upon the above you can see that you will probably end up with at least two rods and reels. The good news is that they will make your fishing experience much more enjoyable; and if you buy quality equipment, it will last you for a very, very long time.

- **School:** The color of the fly line is unimportant since the leader and tippet hide it.

  Dave: I have several different color fly lines and it doesn't seem to affect anything.

- **School:** Deet on the hands ruins a fly line!!!

  Dave: I am very careful if I am using products with Deet; and, whenever I can, I try to pick insect repellant that uses a different ingredient, for example, picaridin.

- **School:** Clean your fly line after using. Use Armor All or water. It makes the line last longer and this is the expensive part of the system.

  Dave: I clean my fly line every so often with dish detergent and rinse it with water. I then dress it with some fly line dressing that I bought for that job. So far my fly lines seem to be in good shape. It's only been a few years, however.

- **School:** The first rod guide is the "stripping guide" because it takes the most wear. It has a ceramic center to make it handle the wear.

  Dave: The other guides are called "snake guides" for obvious reasons. Then there is the Tip-Top guide at the end.

- **School:** Don't use nose oil on the ferrules (the male/female system that holds the multiple pieces of the rod together). This was for metal rods – not graphite.

  Dave: The oil was supposed to make the ferrules easier to take apart. Here is a trick that I learned from somewhere in my travels. If you can't get the rod pieces to come apart, put them behind your knees grabbing each section with your hands. Then use the strength of your legs to pull them apart. I haven't had to do this very often, but it works.

13

- **School:** Snug up ferrules from time-to-time.

  Dave: I must admit that I don't do this very often, but it seems logical, doesn't it?

- **School:** When buying a rod, take your reel with you so that you have that in common with all of them. Try out the rods before buying!!!

  Dave: Since I have always purchased both the rod and the reel at the same time I haven't had to do this. However, it makes sense to me.

- **School:** You will use about six inches per fly tie, so a tippet of 18 to 24 inches is good.

  Dave: I have used three knots to tie my flies to the tippet, the Improved Clinch, the Uni-knot (also called the Duncan Loop) and a knot called the "16-20 knot". All of these knots can be tied so as to lose only three inches of tippet. I am sure that the school was being conservative. Another reason that they might have overestimated at six inches is that the knots are easier to tie when you have a lot of tag end to play with.

- **School:** Test your leader and tippet and fly knots before fishing.

  Dave: I only do this for the fly knot itself and since I use the loop system everywhere else, this is all I really need. I did lose two fish due to a fly knot coming loose even after testing it, however. I don't believe that it was the lack of good testing that did it, but rather the knot that I was using. I saw this neat knot called the "Davey Knot" on the web. Since my name is Dave, why not use my namesake? It was supposed to be easy and fast to tie, and it was. However, I lost two fish while using this knot, so I can't recommend it. By the way, I know that I tied the knot correctly in both cases, so it was the knot.

According to the web article on the Davey Knot, the person recommending it never had a problem, so I don't know what to say other than I'm NOT going to use it anymore. I am going to stick with the 16-20, the Improved Clinch or the Duncan Loop. I haven't had any of these come apart in all of my fishing (both spincasting and fly). As an added observation, if you think about the Improved Clinch knot in terms of what it takes to cause it to come undone, it has what I would call a "backup mechanism" built into the knot. That is, even if the tag end slips back through the last loop in the knot, it still has the first loop that you put the tag through after winding it around the tippet. In fact, without the second loop the knot is called simply the "Clinch Knot." The second loop makes it "Improved." As an engineer, I like this aspect of the knot.

- **School:** If fish are constantly refusing, change something.

  Dave: I agree. The first thing to do is go to a smaller fly. Then, if that doesn't work, try a different pattern (or as I say in the chapter on Nymphing, go to a nymph). One time I wasn't getting any bites until I went to a longer tippet. I guess they didn't like the bulkier part of the leader.

- **School:** Use foam cases for flies; will float if dropped.

  Dave: Amen! Having dropped a couple in the river, I can tell you that this is true. See more on my fly boxes in the Appendix on that subject. By the way, put your name and phone number (or email address) on the box using a permanent marker so the nice person that finds the box can get it back to you.

- **School:** Hold the fly until you are ready to fish. Hold it by the bend.

  Dave: I will usually hook the fly on one of the guides or the hook retainer loop on the rod if I am walking. If I am not moving a long distance then I do what the school recommends.

- **School:** A "Plunge Pool" is good to fish. It is between 2 rapids.

  Dave: In the mountain streams you have lots of pools of various sizes (basketball to small backyard swimming pool). See the Mountain Trout School chapter for what I learned for fishing pools.

- **School:** After two or three casts into the same place, you are wasting your time in most cases.

  Dave: I have found this to be very true. You can, however, sit down and wait for about 10 minutes and try again, especially if you switch from a dry fly to a nymph.

6 Joining Trout Unlimited

Okay, I now know the basics of fly-fishing, but where do I go to fish? I have to admit that this is the main reason that I joined Trout Unlimited (known mostly as "TU"), but since then Trout Unlimited has given me a way to contribute to the community and the environment in a focused way, not to mention the nice people that I have met.

Some examples of TU projects that I think make it worthwhile are listed below. I will expand on them a little bit just to show you that organizations like this are worth your time. Of course, there are others, but I have no experience with them.

You might ask why I don't join more organizations, for example, the International Fly-fishing Association, which is a nonprofit organization concerned with the conservation of all fish, in all waters world-wide. It is a matter of commitment. I have found that I can only focus on a limited set of goals. I would rather do a few things well than a lot of things badly or not at all.

Table 6-1 Trout Unlimited Activities

1. Stream cleanup and restoration (putting in logs, etc. to stabilize the banks)
2. Helping various Virginia governmental agencies with stocking streams
3. Supporting Kids' and Teens' Day at Bon Air Park in Arlington
4. Conservation and Fishing Camp for High School students at Graves' Mountain Lodge in Syria, Virginia
5. Fish With A Member (FWAM) trips twice a month
6. Keeping members aware of legislation that affects fishing environments (and other uses)
7. Monthly meetings with lectures by experts on fly-fishing
8. Campaigns like "Back The Brookie" that seeks to protect the brook trout's habitat.

Now I will pick a couple of items in the table to elaborate on further. First, the FWAM trips are the best way to learn where to fish, but more than that they show you how to get there and where to park. There are some books that say, for example, that you can fish the North Fork of the Shenandoah River at various places near Woodstock, Virginia. However, once you get there you may find that there are only two parking spaces possible and they are not marked at all since they are at the end of a country road.

You have to ask yourself the question "Is it okay to park here, or will some local person not like it?" I found on one trip that there were parking spots galore; but if you parked there, your car could get vandalized. It turns out there was actually only one, or at most, two spots that the locals didn't care about. By going with George Paine on his FWAM trips, I found out about a lot of that kind of important information.

Along with the FWAM trips, the monthly meetings are fun and you eventually get to know some of the members so that you begin to feel like you are a member of a nice family. Everyone that I have met at the meetings has been very nice and helpful. Of course, the speakers give you a lot of information that you especially need when you are beginning. I take tons of notes and then go home and type up expanded versions on my home PC. This is largely how this book came about.

The second TU activity that I would like to talk about is one that I have been involved in these last two years. It is the Kids' and Teens' Day project lead by John Hadley. Programs like the Kids' and Teens' Day will certainly produce some adults who will care about the environment - not just fishing.

Briefly, what we did was to help the Arlington County Park Authority with stocking a local stream called "Four Mile Run" with over 1000 rainbow trout. They purchased them from a hatchery in West Virginia, I am told. After the stocking, we manned a tent to which kids could come for help with rigging up and getting bait. John had packages with various bait, like power bait, plastic worms, etc., and gave them out to anyone who asked.

I and the other TU volunteers did things like taking the "ZEBCO Specials" from KMART or other stores out of their packages and rigging them up. We had hooks, split shot and bobbers available (again John bought them). Since some of the kids did not have any experience with fishing, we sometimes gave them a quick casting lesson. Everyone was very appreciative of our efforts, and it just makes you feel good about yourself.

One funny story that I have to tell on myself is that on the Teens' Day, which was the Thursday before Kids' Day, I realized that I had forgotten how to handle and cast a spincasting outfit. How embarrassing!!! It had been over 15 years since I had spincast and I had forgotten. So in preparation for the following Kids' Day, I got out my old open faced and closed faced spincast rods and practiced casting. It came back almost immediately, but I am sure that I will forget by next year, so I am keeping those two rods to refresh my memory each year.

In case you were wondering, almost everyone was spincasting. I think I only saw one person with a fly rod on Teens' Day. Who cares what they use to catch the fish, it is only important that they catch them!

7 Getting My Waders and Boots

Now I will tell you my wader/boots story. After having taken the introductory school, I was ready to get serious about fly-fishing. It was clear that I was going to have to get some waders and boots, so I went to L. L. Bean in Tyson's Corner, Virginia. It's in the Mall there. It's a very big store (2 levels) and has a small fishing department. The reason that I went to Bean is that I had taken the lunch time casting from them and also the introductory fly-fishing school. In addition, I really like the store.

I talked to someone about waders. Unfortunately, not knowing anything about what I wanted or needed was a real problem. This is always the case for newbies. You are totally blind and have to rely upon the integrity and experience of the salesperson to put you into the gear that is right for you.

The guy that helped me was very nice and I am sure very honest; however, he put me into waders that didn't fit (they didn't have the better size) and recommended rubber-soled shoes.

Now here is an example of how I hope that this book will help you. You simply have to get some advice from people whom you trust BEFORE you buy waders and boots.

It turned out that I went to a Trout Unlimited meeting soon after buying the waders and boots. (Luckily I hadn't used them up to that point; although the great thing about Bean is that you can return anything if you are not satisfied.) Anyway, I talked to several people at Trout Unlimited that same night and determined that felt soles were the way to go. Since I knew that the waders did not fit me as well as I would have liked, I just returned everything and went to Orvis.

It was just the luck of the draw again at Bean, as I have since talked with at least two very knowledgeable salespersons who, I am sure, would have put me into the right gear. In fact, one of the salespersons was a woman who was clearly an expert in fly-fishing and gave me a tip on a caddis fly that has worked great. She also gave me a fishing spot to try on the Rapidan River.

But luck being what it is, I didn't get the person that I needed at Bean when I was shopping for waders. So, as I said, I went elsewhere.

The salesman at Orvis spent an hour with me (this was during the week - gee it's great to be retired). Right off I knew that I was on the right track when he told me that he recommended felt-soled boots (without my telling him that I had been told that at the TU meeting).

7 Getting My Waders and Boots

I tried on some ProGuide 2 waders with very light-weight boots (Note to reader: Get the lightest boots that you can afford because sometimes you are going to have to walk a long ways in them; and heavy boots will wear you out). The ProGuide line was a little more than I wanted to pay (or at the time thought that I needed), but he didn't have my size in the lesser priced model, so I opted for them.

By the way, one of the things that he had me do in order to check the fit of the waders, was to get down on my haunches like I was picking up something from the ground. This tells you whether or not the waders will flex enough and if they are too tight for you. <u>This is a great tip</u>!!!

While I'm at it, I might as well tell you that I have toyed with the idea of getting hip waders or waist waders. My experience is that if you get "breathable" waders that can fold down so that they become waist waders, then that is all you really need. I have never been too hot in my waders, and I especially like the fact that they are high enough so they don't fill with water if I get in too deep, as I have done on several occasions. One time we were restoring a stream, that is, putting in some trees along the bank so it would not erode so fast and also to provide fish habitat. The guys with hip waders couldn't go into the deeper pools. One guy got in a little too deep, nothing dangerous mind you, but water got in over his hips and he was wet from then on.

So, I would say that waist waders are not necessary if you have chest waders that fold down, but hip waders may be useful if you are doing a lot of small stream fishing in the mountains.

Getting back to my wader purchase, at the end of the hour that the salesman spent with me I was very comfortable with the wader fit and the boot choice. I opted for studs thinking that I might need them to not slip on rocks, etc. With a few years under my belt, however, I don't think that I need them, and they can scratch floors and other things too easily. The salesman has since told me that he thinks that they only are useful on a couple of rivers in Pennsylvania. Note to reader: If he had told me this when I chose the studs originally, it probably wouldn't have made any impact with me. <u>I wasn't ready for the information yet</u>. This is what experience buys you. You can judge things more easily. This goes for things that you read in fly-fishing books also. There is so much information out there. What is best for your fishing is only determined by trial and error.

[When I originally wrote this in March of 2006, I hadn't fished without the studs. Since doing so from March to November of 2006, I can say that I do slip more, but not enough to make me want the studs again. I am just aware of the slipping possibility and am more careful.]

With my waders and boots on, I was definitely getting to look like a fly-fisherman even if I didn't know what a brook trout looked like or how to catch one.

8 Catching Fish in Spite of Myself

This chapter will present some important things to remember as a newbie, and will tell you about two fishing trips that illustrate what NOT to do if you want to catch more fish.

Telling you what I did badly on these trips will be, I think, more informative than laying out all of the tricks and techniques that people have found over the years. When you are new to the sport, most of that just doesn't register. However, when I tell you about how I screwed up, it should help you not to do the same.

Actually, what happens is that you may read or watch a video on fly-fishing, and they reel off tons of information. You just can't pick out the stuff that is most important for you at your stage of expertise at that moment in time. Having just gone through that stage, namely, being extremely new, I can hopefully give you information that will make a difference right now.

First, some important things to remember:

Presentation of the fly and not spooking the fish are the two most important aspects of fishing. This is not only my opinion, but also the opinion of others more experienced than I am.

First, I will say a few words about presentation. To present a fly correctly, think of how that fly would act if it were NOT attached to your leader; that is, just floating on the water. More importantly, it would have absolutely no drag due to something holding it back, like your leader. This is what you should strive for in your presentation.

There are several ways to minimize drag, for example, the puddle cast or wiggling the line just before it lands or mending the line. I won't go into them here since they are discussed at length in other books, articles and on the web. Read about drag and other aspects of presentation, but remember only one thing for now, "If the fly looks like it is attached to a line, then you will catch less fish."

Now, how about not scaring fish? A major problem for newbies is scaring the fish away. Use common sense in this regard, for example, don't drag your wading stick in the water. Another example is, don't approach from upstream if you suspect that they are facing that way, unless you are very far away or well off to the side. Also, do not splash the water as you walk if you have to be in the water, which you should avoid on narrow streams. Think of yourself as a heron. They take a soft step and then stop. Look at the water motion that your steps make. If the water disturbance is going out far and rapidly from your leg, then you are signaling your presence to the fish.

Lastly, look at your fly when it lands. Did it splash? If so, then that could have also spooked the fish. Ideally, you want your cast to put the fly line just above where you want it to land and then gently fall to the water.

The above two observations, namely good presentation and being stealthy, are the most important in my opinion. Get them right and you will catch a lot of fish. However, here are some other tips that I have found helpful as well.

- If the fish are fussy (meaning you are not getting bites as opposed to there being no action whatsoever) then try a lighter tippet. This is true, and it is a good tip; however, when you are a newbie, not getting bites is more likely due to your bad presentation or splashing around than fussy fish.
- Use brighter colored flies on overcast day with fast water and/or water that is not clear so that the fish can see them. I have had a lot of luck with flies with flash in them, like a "flashback nymph" or a black Wooly Bugger with some bits of flash.
- Use natural colors like olive for your flies when the water is clear and/or slow. This is because the fish have more of a chance to analyze the fly and are better fooled by something that looks as natural as you can get it.
- If you use floatant, put it only on the fly body, not on the tail so that it can continue to wiggle properly.
- They say that you should observe a pool for 15 minutes before fishing it. I haven't been able to wait that long (I don't have a lot of patience), but I do look at it for a little while prior to starting. By the way, one day a short time ago when I was walking a stream near my house (without any fishing gear), I was surprised at how the pool changed the longer I watched. It was like a different pool altogether. I could see fish and other things that I couldn't see when I first looked at it. So what they told me is really the best thing to do. I will try to do better in the future.
- If you do look at a pool before fishing, observe what the fish are doing and the bug activity at the site. What color are the bugs; what size? Are the fish top feeding; any rings? Pick up a rock and look at the nymphs. Observe their size and color. It's fun!
- Watch for the foam line in the stream. The saying "Foam Is Home" is really true! This is where there will be fish eating bugs that are coming down the faster moving water. It is also a low energy place; that is, the fish doesn't have to expend a lot of energy to feed. This, of course, is assuming that the surface currents are the same as the rest of the water column. A lot of times it is not.
- The fish will be facing upstream (unless they are in an eddy or something that causes them to face in a different direction), so cast above them. Ideally, you want to be below the fish so that they don't see you. At a recent TU meeting I saw a very interesting and

informative film that showed fish underwater in various situations. What surprised me was that they were facing in all different directions. This was because the bottom currents were different from the surface currents due to obstructions. So I guess that the fish facing upstream is a good general rule, but not hard and fast.
- One time on a FWAM trip, a senior member of TU told me that my leader was too long. This was while I was making a very short cast. This begged the question "Do I have to carry long and short leaders?" My experience is that you just cut it if it is too long and add some tippet if it is too short. This is why you really need to be able to tie knots fast. This is also an advantage to the loop system for leaders, fly line, etc. (See elsewhere in the book for more discussion on this subject.)
- As a result of the sun beating down on the back of my neck, I decided that I needed a hat with a flap on the back. This also helps with insects if they are a problem.
- I have bought a pair of very light gloves that have no covering for the fingers above the knuckle, and I really like them. They let me do everything that I need to do, like stripping line and tying knots. They also give me a better grip on the fish without having to put as much pressure on it. Still wet your hands before handling the fish, however.

Okay, with the above tips firmly in place, let's see how I managed to forget them all when I went on my first non-panfish fishing trips. I say "non-panfish" because panfish, like bluegills and their cousins can be caught even violating everything that I have told you above including splashing and a bad presentation. This is why I love them and go back to them often to boost my ego when the other fish are rejecting me.

8.1 My First Brookie

My first trip with the Trout Unlimited Saturday group was to the Lower Piney River. It comes out of the Shenandoah Mountains and you can get to it just north of Sperryville after driving south from Warrenton, Virginia.

The Saturday that we went was pretty nice, albeit cloudy and somewhat cool. We arrived at where we were going to park at about 10 A.M. What I said about knowing the parking situation before arriving really applied here. Our Trout Unlimited FWAM leader, George Paine knew this and we only had three cars. There was space for two at a small area that was public, but the third car had to park off the road in a non-public area. I mean it was close to a public area, but anywhere off the road was not public. It wasn't posted, but you can still get into trouble with the locals if you park where they don't want you to park.

George got permission for the third car to park and we were set.

It is a little bit of a walk to get to the Shenandoah State Park boundary where you can legally fish, so having my lightweight boots really helped. The waders worked well too. They were comfortable, light and flexible. No problem for the walk.

George and I talked while walking. I picked his brain for fishing tips and such. He is a very nice guy and eager to help newbies like me. That goes for other members of Trout Unlimited also. In fact I rode down with two guys, and I picked their brains too. I have always been that way and it has served me well in getting myself up to a reasonable level of expertise as rapidly as possible. I hope that I can do the same for others. This book is my first payback to all of those who have helped me so far.

Okay, I put on my waders and boots at the car like everyone else was doing. Some rigged up their rods. George and I didn't. We then walked up the road until there was a crossing over the Piney and continued up the trail until we were in the Shenandoah National Forest. There was a sign that told us this.

I should tell you that another time when I went fishing by myself to the Piney, I just entered the Piney at the crossing point. I caught a lot of fish including smallmouth bass in a deep pool. I could see houses along the river and wondered about it. Being in the river, I didn't see any postings of NO FISHING or POSTED, but maybe I would have if I had been walking on the banks. In any event, I later found out that this was private property and so I won't be doing that again. The lesson to be learned is to know what is public and what is private, relative to fishing access. Luckily, I didn't see anyone all the time I was fishing; but it could have been a problem, I guess.

Now back to the first Piney trip. After getting to the public access part, we peeled off to fish. I went with George farther up the river and finally we stopped at an old wooden bridge. George was going to fish there, so I went up a little farther.

I rigged up and fished for about an hour with no success. I really didn't have a clue as to what I was doing at this point in the game, so it was no wonder that I didn't have any luck.

About that time, George had worked his way up to me. I was going to fish a pool and I told him about my bad luck (although it really wasn't bad luck, just bad technique). I forget what fly I was using, but George recommended a # 16 Mr. Rapidan dry fly with a yellow parachute (This is a part of the fly that sticks up out of the water so that you can see it better. The fish are looking up and don't see this part of the fly so it doesn't affect its allure to them, but it does let you follow it on the water better.). He gave me one from his flybox and I tied it on. He then told me to flip it up to where the water comes into the pool, so that it looked like it was being carried down by the water.

I did that a couple of times and got a strike! I pulled in a nice size bookie, like the one shown below that I caught later at the Mountain Trout School. My first brook trout!!! I was now an official fly-fisherman! What was even better was that George witnessed my success, so there was backup when I told the others at the end of the day.

Figure 8-1 Shenandoah Mountain Brook Trout

By the way, I released the trout that day as I have released all of the fish that I have caught up to this point in time. Almost all of them swam away under their own power. I love these little fish, and so I am very careful with them and do everything that I can not to harm them.

George left me to continue his fishing and I continued mine. I did not catch another fish that day, but that was okay with me. The thrill of my first wild trout catch was enough for the time being.

At the end of the day, we all compared notes. It turns out that no one had a lot of luck. I think that only one person caught three brookies, and he had changed over to a nymph. Remember that!!! A nymph!!!

Of course, at this point in my fly-fishing education, I didn't comprehend the utility of nymph fishing when top water was not producing fish. But the fact that he had caught some brookies on a nymph, some later literature discussions, and the mountain trout school, caused me to try it. I now use it as my primary fishing technique. See the chapter on Nymphing for more on that subject.

Since the purpose of the book is to get you up to speed on fly-fishing by learning from my mistakes (and hopefully some successes), let me give you some observations about the Lower Piney trip. First of all, in retrospect, I was probably scaring away any potential fish. I did not sneak up on them, I splashed when I waded into a pool, and I am sure that my fly hit the water like a ton of bricks. You just can't do that and expect to catch fish. By the way, I have since learned to avoid going into the water at all cost unless it is really necessary. It is okay for wide rivers, but you don't want to do it on narrow mountain trout streams.

The most important thing that George showed me that day was to toss the fly very softly up to where the brookie was waiting (This is called his "feeding station."). Learn this lesson well! Note that you probably won't use the classic Hollywood fly-cast in the mountains due to all of the overhang. You will end up just flicking the fly to where you want it to go. This is why I bought my 3 weight rod. It is 6 foot 10 inch rather than 9 foot long, thereby letting me keep out of the overhead more easily.

An important lesson learned from the Lower Piney trip was the following. I am sure that the type of fly was a factor; but more importantly, it was the fact that I placed the fly where the fish would naturally expect one to be coming down. It does no good to cast to a place where there are no fish. You can have the best technique and the perfect fly, but the fish just won't be there to see the fly and appreciate your perfect casting form.

8.2 My First Smallie (on a fly)

Here is my second "What Not to Do" trip for your education. It was another TU outing that George took us on down to the North Fork of the Shenandoah River near Edinburg, Virginia. We first stopped at Murray's Fly Shop (and Pharmacy). That was where I first met Harry Murray. He was very nice and eager to tell us what the fish were biting on that Saturday morning. I think that I picked up my first "Strymph" on that visit, and maybe my first leadeyed hellgrammite. The Strymph that Harry created is supposed to imitate either a streamer (minnow, crayfish, leech, etc.) or a nymph, hence the name strymph. As a side note, I was still using my 5 weight rod at this time.

George dropped some of the group off at Chapman's Landing, but I ended up with the others at a different part of the river which was a little farther upstream from there. Upon entering the river, some of us went upstream and some down.

I had ridden down with a guy who was a very experienced bass fly-fisherman. He and I went down the river.

I was using the strymph and had no luck for the first few hours or so. I decided to go a lot farther downstream. I saw a pool and cast into it. I caught a nice sized bluegill. Well, that made my day since I wasn't going to be totally skunked, which is always nice. I made several more casts. Note that these were classic fly casts, that is, full back and forward motion. I was out in the middle of the river, so I didn't have to worry about overhead obstacles like up in the Shenandoah Mountain streams.

I caught another bluegill and then a medium size (about 9 inch) smallmouth bass. That was it for the day (about 5 hours of fishing). I was satisfied and quite pleased with myself until I talked to one of the other guys who had gone upstream when we entered the river. He had caught 10 fish on a Muddler Minnow. He loves this fly. I thought: "Darn, if only I had used the Muddler, I would have caught more fish." Not true!!! At that point in my experience, three fish was doing well. In fact, looking back on the day, I was lucky to catch any fish. Thank goodness for the bluegills!

Okay, what can you learn from this trip? The main thing was that I was again making a lot of noise with my wading. This was the same problem I had with the Lower Piney trip. Luckily, the North Fork is wider than the streams in the mountains and has a lot more ambient noise so my noise was less of a factor; however, I am sure that I still scared away a lot of fish that day.

Another lesson learned was that I was not casting to where the fish would most likely be. Again, this was the same problem I had at the Lower Piney. I should have chosen to cast where the riffles were and along the banks. In fact, I caught the smallie under a big tree that had fallen into the river. For smallies, this is good cover from predators and provides shade. Always, fish in places like that. Remember that a streamer is not fished on top of the water, so get it down to the bottom and drag it along like it is a crayfish or other food item. You can also swim it like a minnow would do.

You will read in just about any book on fly-fishing that the "Across and Down" cast is a good one. This is true for situations like the North Fork. Stand on the side of the river and cast across (or maybe slightly upstream). Let the streamer settle to the bottom or near it. Then start stripping fly line so that it comes back to you while being swept downstream. It will swing across and cover a lot of territory. What you are looking for is a fish that is somewhere along its path as the line is being retrieved.

A question naturally arises. "Should you be above the fish where they can see you rather than in back of them where they can't?" The "Across and Down" cast is only for relatively wide rivers where the potential fish are far enough away from you that they will most likely not see you. Also, the "Across" part of the retrieve is pretty far away from you, and this is the major part of the cast that will catch fish.

To give you an idea of just how far I have come since that first trip, I have gone back to that part of the river at least 20 times since then. I have consistently caught over ten fish and several times I left because it was getting too easy, having caught over twenty really good sized fish, both smallies and fallfish. I even tried a Muddler Minnow, but didn't have much luck with it. My go-to streamer for this type of fishing is a black leadeyed hellgrammite! It has two things going for it. One, the leadeye gets it down to where the fish are even in fast water; and two, it just looks like something that a fish would want to eat.

9 Mountain Trout Saturday Class and School

9.1 Mountain Trout Saturday Class

On a Saturday in March 2005 I went to a Trout Fishing Class held by Harry Murray at his place in Edinburg, Virginia. It was very informal with some folding chairs set up off to the side of his pharmacy/fly shop.

Knowing that I was going to be able to ask questions to an acknowledged leader in the field of fly-fishing, I went prepared with a list of questions. I have always done this before meetings since I get a lot more out of the sessions if I have thought about the subject beforehand. Another advantage in preparing my questions in advance was that I was able to ask more questions than the rest of the class put together. How many times have you returned home after a meeting and thought of many more questions that you would have liked to have asked?

So, I had my questions and Harry had the answers and/or a lot of good tips. I will now share them with you. I will insert my comments in parentheses, if I have any. By the way, if you are not familiar with one or more terms, for example, "Swing Nymphing," which is a Harry Murray technique, just look them up on the web. Google is such a great invention!!!

1. **Question:** What is the proper reel drag?
   Answer: You use the lightest drag for mountain trout. About 1/2 of what is needed for a larger fish since you will use your hand on the line for the rest of the drag.
2. **Question:** Why would I want to use a Mr. Rapidan Dry Fly (invented by Harry) relative to a classic Adams, that is, what is it giving me that the Adams won't?
   Answer: The Adams is a great fly; however, it has a gray body and most of Virginia stream insects are brown. It works, however. (I, that is, the author, can personally vouch for that!) Note, the Adams doesn't look like anything in particular. Another fly like this is the Royal Wulff. It just looks like something that the fish think is good to eat.
3. **Question:** How do you set the depth in nymph fishing?
   Answer: It is a lot of guessing and "feel." With "Swing Nymphing" it is less of a problem as you let it sink and then lift the rod as it comes to you from your upstream cast.
4. **Question:** What do you do when you get a fly caught on something, and you want to retrieve it, but don't want to mess up the fishing spot by scaring all of the fish away (sometimes referred to as "putting down the pool")?
   Answer: Try a roll cast, then pull the line straight towards you (don't bend the rod or you might break it). Then if it doesn't come loose, you have to make a decision to lose

the fly and keep the pool or vice versa. (I have used the roll cast trick many times. It works! You can also let out a lot of line and try to work your way around to the other side of the obstacle. I have done this twice to retrieve a fly.)

5. **Question:** Do studs make noise?
   Answer: Yes, so be very careful, but Harry uses them.
6. **Question:** Do you really need all those flies?
   Answer: You can get away with the Mr. Rapidan dry fly during hatches, the Mr. Rapidan Emerger (imitates Quill Gordon and another fly) for nymphing and the Strymph for streamer. (I like the Hare's Ear Nymph myself.)
7. **Question:** Where do you put a split shot if you are using one?
   Answer: For nymphing put a spit shot about 6 inches up from the fly (I like it a little farther up, say, about 9 to 12 inches). You can put the split shot in a bag of water overnight to get the shine off of it. (I have found that if the split shot is too shiny then the fish go after it instead of the nymph. Also, tungsten shot is shiny, but better for the environment than lead, so I use it. It is more expensive, however.) Don't use any shot larger than a BB size or it will scare the fish.
8. **Tip:** When walking down from a parking lot on Skyline Drive to a stream, go farther down and fish going back up to the lot.
9. **Tip:** Fish want to be near to the current for food, but protected from it. Therefore look for the place where the fast water meets the slower water. (Remember: "Foam is Home.")
10. **Tip:** The magic temperature for trout is 40 degrees! Therefore the later part of March is when things start to get going for dry flies. Up to that point, you can use nymphs. When the fish start feeding on top water insects such as mayflies, you can use dry flies like the Mr. Rapidan dry fly #14 in early spring to mid-May and then go to #16 after that. Use darker colors and larger flies to begin with and get lighter and smaller later in the season. (Because that is what the insects do).
11. **Tip:** In the fall after the hatches, use midges, ants, beetles and other terrestrials. (The Mr. Rapidan flying beetle looks like a lot of things and I have had a lot of success with it.)
12. **Tip:** Harry did an experiment on the number of fish caught per hour versus water temperature and found a sharp rise at 42 degrees up to about 52 degrees and then dropping off as the temperature approached 62 degrees. He got eight fish/hour at 48 degrees. As the temperature rises, so does the trout's metabolism, and therefore they need more food. The insects hatch at these temperatures.
13. **Tip:** Come up to a pool and fish the close parts first. So fish just up from the lip (where the pool empties into the next riffle). Sneak in behind boulders or otherwise try to hide yourself as much as you can.
14. **Tip:** A fish rise form looks like a BB thrown into the pool.
15. **Tip:** Use longer casts (and longer, finer tippet) in low water because the fish are spookier. More stealth is needed!

16. **Tip:** In the spring, if the water levels are too high, fish the upper part of the stream rather than the lower part. For example, go to Skyline Drive and walk down to the Rose River rather than entering it at its lower accesses. (By the way, this is why people have given the names "Lower Piney" and "Upper Piney" to parts of the Piney River.)
17. **Tip:** Larger streams have more water and are broader, therefore usually have less spooky fish. Use larger flies in larger streams and use the across cast and let it drift downstream. A #10 Olive Strymph works well on larger streams as a minnow imitator. (Like I said before, I love the leadeyed Hellgramite when I am fishing for smallmouth bass, although I have had a lot of luck with the Strymph as well.) Using the across and down cast, you can walk down the river. This works in wide rivers, but not in narrow streams due to the shorter casts in the narrow streams. (Note that you are above the fish when walking down the river. It is okay for the larger streams and rivers. Don't try this for small narrow streams, or at least make longer presentations.)
18. **Tip:** For streamers, cast across and down about a 10 degree angle and strip to work the streamer across the bottom. Then step downstream a step or so and do it again. This will show the streamer to as many fish in the area as possible.
19. **Tip:** In winter, you can fish spring-fed streams because the water will be about 50 degrees near where the spring exits even if the water is 36 degrees elsewhere. Cast near the spring exit. Look for vegetation to indicate the spring exit.
20. **Tip:** In November and December, you will see "Cress Bugs" in size #14 and #16 on a spring fed creek.
21. **Tip:** Use a 9 foot 4X leader in the spring and a 9 foot 6X leader in summer. An approximate formula for the leader size is: Leader Size = Fly Size/3. For example, #14/3 = 4.6 => 4X.
22. **Tip:** Harry doesn't like the Wooly Bugger because it is tied with a Marabou tail that bunches up over itself like an umbrella when it gets wet and doesn't look like anything. Harry uses the Strymph instead. (I have found the Wooly Bugger to be very effective, however.)
23. **Tip:** Red Squirrel Nymph is a good generic nymph. (I love this fly.)
24. **Tip:** Royal Wulff is a good attractor (#12 and #14). (I haven't caught anything on a Wulff up to this time, but that could be due to a lot of things.)
25. **Tip:** If trout refuse flies, try an ant. Fish love ants falling from trees.
26. **Tip:** The "parachute" on the fly is so that you see it better. The hook bend weight keeps it upright.
27. **Tip:** Harry recommends a Mr. Rapidan Emerger for early spring.
28. **Tip:** The Shenk's cricket matches mountain wasps and is good for searching.
29. **Tip:** Drag is a big problem. If the fly is going too fast, the trout will not take it.
30. **Tip:** Fish will usually not be in "dead water" because there is no food there.
31. **Tip:** After June 1st, Harry tries to spot a fish in water and get into position. He then counts to 30. If the fish hasn't moved, then you haven't spooked him.
32. **Tip:** He doesn't use double taper lines anymore.

33. **Tip:** By mashing down the barb, you have a better chance of fully hooking the fish rather than just getting it on the hook point. (I always mash down my barbs.)
34. **Tip:** Dip fly into liquid fly floatant. (I use paste floatant. I put some between my fingers, let it melt due to my body heat and then put it on the fly.) You can swish the fly in the water before casting it if you want, but I figure that the first cast will do that anyway.
35. **Tip:** Be careful with suntan lotion. It will destroy fly lines!!!
36. **Tip:** Harry uses a Falstaff staff <u>with large diameter shaft</u>. He said that the thinner ones can be dangerous since they bend more easily. (I use a regular walking stick.)
37. **Tip:** With knotted leader, cut above the last knot to replace or change the tippet. (See my section on leaders. I don't use knotted leaders and don't recommend them, especially for a newbie.)
38. **Tip:** Knots hang in lily pads and pickup algae, so knotless leaders may be better there. (This is Harry's statement, not mine, but I agree with him.)
39. **Tip:** Harry uses a Needle knot for the fly line to the leader. (A Nail knot is a good substitute, but put some Pliobond on it to make it slide through the guides better. The Needle knot has the advantage of symmetry since the leader comes out of the center of the flyline rather than the side. I would still use some Pliobond on the Needle knot, however.)

9.2 Mountain Trout School

One of the best experiences that I have had so far in my fly-fishing learning process has been the Mountain Trout School that I took in early April 2005.

Figure 9-1 A Pool in the Blue Ridge Mountains at Trout School

It was taught by Jeff Murray, who is the son of Harry Murray. Jeff is a very accomplished fly-fisherman in his own right, so I was learning from a master of the sport. The school was given over a two day period. Here is what the advertisement on Harry's website "www.murraysflyshop.com" has to say about the school. Note that the costs are as of April 2005.

"Our Mountain Trout Schools are held in the Shenandoah National Park, which is 40 miles east of our fly shop. These schools cover casting, entomology, reading the water, proper fly selection, and how to fish dry's, nymphs, and streamers for trout in freestone streams. Many of the fine points covered in my book, Trout Fishing in the Shenandoah National Park ($11.95) are covered in detail in these schools. All schools are held on Weekdays. Cost: $325.00 per person

These schools are the best way for anyone to learn to fly fish or to brush up on their technique. Almost the entire time in these schools is spent on the stream fishing so even beginners come away with a thorough understanding of the art of fly angling. Schools start at 9 a.m. with a slide show, then drive to the stream and fish until 5 p.m. each day. You will spend approximately one hour in the classroom and the rest of the time on the stream where you can practice what you would like to learn with the help of one-on-one sessions with our guides/instructors."

I can tell you that I was drinking from the firehose during the lectures as Jeff really gives you a lot of information. As usual, I took up a lot of the class with my questions. Again, I am like a sponge around knowledgeable people like Jeff and, since I am paying them to be there, I am going to extract as much information as I can from them. Jeff was great in answering all of my questions and tolerating my ignorance.

As the advertisement above said, you get one-on-one instruction when you are on the stream. Jeff watched me for about a half hour on each of the two days that I was on the stream. I caught several fish during that time. It is extremely instructive to have someone tell you what you should do and/or are doing incorrectly right there when you are fishing. I learned a lot!!!

I don't know where the class is being held now, but when I went it was at the Graves' Mountain Lodge in Syria, Virginia. This is a wonderful place to stay if you want to be near the Shenandoah Mountains and all of the fishing places that are at its base, for example, Oak Creek Canyon, the Rapidan, the Hughes and the Rose. In fact, the Rose River runs right in front of the Lodge.

Now back to my Mountain Trout School experience. I had bought Harry's book on the subject so I had prepared a load of questions to ask Jeff when he came to that point in the lecture, just like I had done for his father's Saturday class. It also helped me to really understand what Jeff was saying since it was not the first time that I had been exposed to the material.

As I have done previously with the L. L. Bean School and the Saturday Class, I am going to simply give you my notes that I took while at the school (in a less cryptic form, of course), rather than write a narrative. This will give you the most information with the least amount of reading. I will also give you my later thinking based upon my experience since the school. I will preface my original notes with "School" to emphasize that this is what I got from the class in contrast to what I may be doing now. Where needed I will preface my current thinking with "Dave."

Table 9-1   Mountain Trout Fishing School Notes April 11, 2005

General Notes

- **School:** Loop-to-loop connections are great!!! Especially when you have forgotten to put on strike indicators higher up on the leader. You don't have to cut off your nymph. You can just take off the tippet loop and slide them on from that end.

- **School:** You can use split shot about eight inches (the Orvis book says about twelve inches, and Harry in his Saturday class said six inches, so try them all and see what works for you.) above the nymph, then indicators two feet and four feet above the nymph.

  Dave: I have found that I don't need strike indicators at all by using the Leisenring Lift technique, which can be found in many books and on the web, if you are interested. I may miss fish, but I still catch a lot of them. Just watch your line very carefully, especially if it is somewhat curled from being on the reel.

I have read in some books that some experts don't recommend strike indicators since they make you too dependent on them. However, if you do need an indicator, put one somewhere on the line where you can see it when the nymph is on the bottom. This may take some trial and error to get it at the right spot. Harry and, of course, Jeff use a lot of indicators at various distances from the fly. I find that it gets too confusing having too many indicators, especially if you are using bright red leaders like they do. You have to be very disciplined in watching the appropriate indicator when more than one is used.

Personally, I have gone to standard <u>no-color</u>, <u>unknotted</u> leaders with no strike indicator. However, remember that I am a newbie and they are experts with years of experience. It may well be that I will change my opinion as I gain experience, but for now I catch fish with what I am doing and it's simpler for me.

- **School:** The key to nymphing is to keep the rod tip ahead of the indicators; watch the one that is out of the water unless the one in the water is very visible; if an indicator twitches or even stops, set the hook!!!

  Dave: Since I use the Leisenring Lift technique, I am tight to the nymph all the time and can feel the strike. A similar technique is Harry's "swing nymphing."

- **School:** If the pool is not producing fish, it is possible that you have spooked them and don't know it. Move on to next pool.

  Dave: There have been several occasions when I wasn't catching anything, and in fact, didn't see any action at all, only to find that I was following someone up the stream. Look for footprints or other indicators of previous people spoiling the pools. If you don't see any indicators, but see absolutely no action, then suspect that others have been there. This may not be the case, but it is a good guess.

- **School:** Try to release the fish in the lower pool so that you don't mess up the current pool.

  Dave: I agree that this is nice to do from a fishing standpoint; however you have to keep moving down to the lower pool to do it AND you are screwing up the fish's life by moving it out of its territory. I just live with the pool being messed up if it turns out to be that way. I have been told by some other experienced individuals that most people don't get more than one fish out of a pool anyway, so just release the fish in his pool, try to catch other fish in that pool, and if there is no more action, go to the next one.

- **School:** Little vertical strips on the belly of a brookie indicate that it is not an adult yet; that is, it is less than a year old.

- **School:** The headwater of the Upper Rapidan is a Type 1 stream (Hydrologist term). A stream going through flat land is called a Type 2. One that is just above flowing into the Chesapeake Bay is Type 3.

- **School:** Mountain Freestone streams have about 175 pounds of food per acre of stream bottom due to the pH of the streams. They are somewhat acid, therefore have less insect hatches. The Shenandoah streams have pHs of around 7 to 7.3. The only alkalinity we get is from leaves and other decaying matter. Acid rain doesn't help either. A pH of 6.5 (like near coal mines) is deadly.

  Dave: To give you concrete number, I was at the Hughes River on one occasion and measured a pH of 6.8.

- **School:** Spring creeks have 2000 pounds of food per acre of stream bottom. An example is Mossy Creek. Spring creeks are coming through limestone, so they have a pH of about 7.8, which is great for the fish and the bugs that they live on.

- **School:** In the spring, the Upper Rapidan and others will not have extremely spooky fish, so you can get away with a non-cautious approach. In lower water levels, this is not the case!!!

- **School:** Lots of dimples on water mean fish are taking insects at the surface film without breaking it.

- **School:** Jeff recommends that you fish from the Skyline Drive part of the stream when the water is high and come in from below when the water is low.

- **School:** If you are getting refusals and/or the water is low, try a smaller tippet.

- **School:** Midges are a good fly for late summer or early fall. Fish will sometimes lock in on midges and not be interested in an ant or cricket. Try 7x tippet and a #18, then a #20 midge if the #18 doesn't produce anything. Midges are out there about any time of year on any river. They look like mosquitoes. Very seldom are all pools feeding on midges, so go to another pool if the current one has no action.

- **School:** Trout are in their eggs for about 100 days.

Dry Fly-fishing Notes
- **School:** There are four steps to successful mountain trout fishing (with one more for nymph fishing).

    o Read the water to find the fish **feeding stations.**
    o Use a **cautious** approach.
    o Give an **accurate presentation** of the fly (teacup accuracy for basketball size pools relative to bathtub accuracy for a larger river like the North Fork).
    o Use a **drag-free** drift for dry fly-fishing (keep rod tip up in the air and watch the fly to see that it is just floating on the water - not being pulled by the leader).
    o Keep **tight** to the nymph for nymph fishing.

- **School:** One-handed casting works well for dry fly-fishing or nymph fishing.

    Dave: I use this technique a lot, especially in short cast situations.

- **School:** Fish aim into the current that they are experiencing at their water level (which of course may not be what you see on top). In some cases, this could mean that they are facing you as you approach from downstream.

- **School:** A pool has the following identifiable parts: Lip (where the water flows into the next pool), Tail (just above the lip), Mid-Section, Corners (small back-eddies), Head (where the water comes in from the previous pool), Big back-eddies.

- **School:** Fish to the first fish that you could spook. This means that you should fish from the tail to the head of the pool.

  Dave: See what I said previously about usually not being able to catch more than one fish per pool unless you are very skilled like Harry and Jeff.

- **School:** There are several things that a fish needs. Two very important requirements are shelter from overhead predators and food. So there may be a great boulder for protection over in the corner of a pool, but if there is no food there, then there will probably be no fish there.

- **School:** You usually have no fly line out of the tip guide for mountain trout fishing as you try to get as close to the pool as you can without spooking the fish. You fish with mostly leader. The reason is that you can't keep the leader out of the water for a drag-free presentation with any fly line on the water.

- **School:** Keep as little tippet on the water as possible (it also helps with setting the hook because they are quick!!!). Let the fly just float and bounce on the water as it would naturally.

  Dave: Remember what I said in another part of the book about trying to make the fly appear as though it is NOT ATTACHED to the tippet!

- **School:** Don't fish when the brook trout are spawning, roughly from the middle of October to the middle of November. (Check the dates at the local fly shop to exact dates). Go after something else during that time.

- **School:** Try to spot the fish (rises, shadow, dimples on pool).

- **School:** The pool's mid-section is not as productive due to lack of cover, but fish it anyway. Cover the water.

- **School:** An exception to the mid-section lack of production can be if it contains a big rock that causes the food to eddy, just circling for a good while.

- **School:** A twelve inch brookie is a whale for the Shenandoah streams. Nine inch is large. Typical is three to six inches. (Dave: By the way, an interesting fact, at least to me, is that a brook trout is a char like the Alaska char.) Brookies have light spots on a dark background. Rainbows or Browns (true trout) have dark spots on a light background. Brook trout live between three to five years

Dave: I was up in New Jersey one time and a spincaster caught a twelve inch brook trout shown in the figure below. These were stocked trout, however. They were put there for a tournament along with rainbows and browns. The biggest brook trout that I have ever caught has been nine inches, so I originally didn't think that the fish in the photo was indeed a brookie. However, look at the light spots on a dark background. I am pretty sure that it is a brookie. Native mountain brookies in our area, however, look more like the one in the photo in my chapter on catching my first brookie.

Figure 9-2 A 12 Inch Brook Trout

- **School:** Get your hand wet before handling the fish. You don't want to remove a lot of the slime that covers fish because this is part of the fish's defense mechanism. For example, it protects it from harmful bacteria.

- **School:** Watch for wet boot prints to avoid fishing behind someone. You have to wait about 12 hours after a pool is ruined (a common term is "put down") in the spring. Later it is more like 24 hours.

- **School:** If the current is all moving in the same direction, you can just cast up and won't get drag. The drag problem in normal situations is due to multiple directions and speeds of the currents.

- **School:** Any water that is the size of a basketball and contains flat water is classified by Jeff as a "pool."

- **School:** For dry flies, don't cast into the froth since it is mostly air and will sink your fly (it's like a washing machine washing the floatant off the fly). You will probably need to redress it soon after it gets churned up in the water. This is not the case for nymphs!!! You can drop the nymph right into the middle of the froth and be okay. It's better at the fast/slow boundary, however.

- **School:** Mayflies are the only fly that molts once before becoming an adult, therefore there is a dun and a spinner.

- **School:** 85% of a brook trout's caloric intake is nymphs. Nymphing is great for February fishing (33 degrees).

    Dave: This is why I prefer nymph fishing at this stage of my expertise. It is simply easier to catch fish, plus I don't have to remember all of that "Match the Hatch" stuff.

- **School:** Fish nymphs at the slow to fast water line at the head of the pool.

- **School:** If the heads and tails of a pool run together there is too much water for dry fly-fishing. Try the corners and other flat water that you can find. Nymphs are okay, however.

    Dave: Nymphs again!!!

- **School:** Current acts like a funnel and decreases in force the deeper you go.

- **School:** Later in the year you really need to spot the fish (middle of May and later).

- **School:** Brookies will feed on terrestrials all year long, but mostly after the later part of May/first part of June until the frost kills the insects. In the later part of September, it is almost all terrestrials. Also, the fish cruise for the food as opposed to earlier in the year, so try to place the fly in front of them.

- **School:** For refusals, try a smaller fly, then finer tippet, then go to an even smaller fly or just forget that particular fish.

Nymph and Streamer Fishing Notes
- **School:** Any pool that you can get your indicator and fly into at the same time can be nymph fished.

  Dave: Think about that statement relative to dry fly-fishing!

- **School:** A Blue Quill Nymph has three tails, the Quill Gordon has two and there is quite a size difference between the two.

  Dave: On one trip I turned over a rock on the Hughes River and saw a Quill Gordon Nymph. It indeed had the two tails; it also had six bent legs and was the size of my fingernail in length.

- **School:** Murray's Mr. Rapidan dry imitates several mayflies (as seen by the fish from below!). It has moose body hair in the tail (it's a hollow hair which helps maintain buoyancy). It uses a synthetic dubbing for the body, which doesn't absorb water much - therefore good for floating). It has a grizzly hackle (part of the fly that fans out around its body). It has a yellow cattail just to be able to see it. Its parachute has just one wing sticking up; traditional dry flies have two.

  Dave: Any choice of fly is just a personal preference, so don't key in on any particular design. Just find one that works for you. Also, don't get confused by all of the fly-tying terms, like "parachute" or "hackle". Forget it for now and go back later when you want to know more about flies.

- **School:** Mountain streams don't lend themselves well to streamers since streamers are usually fished across and down, and the mountain streams are not wide enough. The fish can see you when it's not wide enough from where you are casting.

- **School:** Fish a streamer between the fast and slow water like a nymph. For example, cast into the edge of a riffle and let it go downstream.

- **School:** Streamer fishing, when it is applicable on a mountain stream, is good for high water and to cover a lot of water. Cast and walk down. A Wooly Bugger is the most popular streamer. A size 8 for trout is as big as you want to use. You should fish streamers on the bottom so use several split shots to get it down.

10 Shad Fiasco and Redemption

On April 27, 2005, I went to the Conowingo Dam in Maryland to fish for the shad that come up the river to spawn. I was to be with a long time friend of the family, Bobby D'Esposito. Bob is an expert fisherman and I figured he could teach me a lot. He invited me up to the dam for a day's fishing and afterwards to go to a cottage to which he had access for the night. We could then fish the next day before returning home.

I left the house at 9:45 in the morning, arrived at the dam at 11: 35. It is 95 miles. I fished all day with no luck. I threw a Mickey Finn, a White Zonker, a Joe's Popper, a Black Wooly with flash, and a flash back nymph. Bobby caught 18 fish on a chartreuse "darter" (See I told you he was an expert!). It has a round head and a wiggly flat tail. It is about two inches long. The fish were jumping all around me, but wouldn't bite. Guys were fishing all the way up to near the dam and pulling them in left and right. I was very disappointed.

At the end of the day, I told Bobby that I was not going to take him up on his cottage offer as I didn't think that I would have any luck the next day. I just wanted to get home to lick my wounds.

After a good night's sleep, and mentally recovered from my skunking by the fish at the dam, I went to talk to Newell Steele at The Angler's Lie, a fly shop in Arlington, Virginia. He said the fish that I saw jumping were acting out part of their mating ritual, not biting on bait. Actually, there is a lot of bait for them to eat if they wanted to, but shad don't eat it during spawning per studies of their stomachs. Well, that was interesting, but why I hadn't I caught any?

As far as my not even getting any bites at the dam, he said that what I needed was a sinking line or tip to get the fly down in the water column where the shad were. My floating line was only getting down to whatever the leader was giving me, maybe about nine feet at most; however, the fish were much deeper than that. I was simply nowhere near where the fish were, other than when they were jumping to show off for the females, I guess.

Boy, did I feel dumb. <u>Learn this lesson from my mistake</u>. Go to a flyshop or talk to someone who knows what they are doing before trying anything well beyond your expertise. It will save you a lot of frustration, not to mention time and energy.

By the way, Newell had come to a Trout Unlimited meeting awhile back and had said everything in that meeting that would have saved me from the skunking. I was at the meeting. I took notes and everything, but it was just a case of being too new to even understand what he was saying. I heard the words, but they didn't register because I had no point of reference. This is often the case when you are a newbie, and I don't know what to tell you other than it is just part of the learning process. Hopefully, my shad story <u>will register</u> with you if you decide to go after them.

The table below summarizes what I know about sinking tips and lines. Even though I have not fished a full sinking line for very long, I am including it in the table because I have learned something important about them, which also applies to the sinking tip. It turns out that the full sinking line casts about the same as a floating line with the sinking tip attached to it, but allows me to get further down in the water column since the full line is 100 feet rather than the sinking tip's 12 feet. I have caught ten Hickory shad on it as of this writing. [Since originally writing this, I have caught many more shad.]

Table 10-1 Sinking Tips and Sinking Lines

Sinking Tip Leaders
- It is needed to get down into the water column. (A floating line will only get you down to about whatever the leader will give you, assuming that you have a heavy fly and/or have weighted it.)
- It is a "poor man's/woman's" sinking line alternative. (A sinking tip will cost less, around $13 versus around $70 for a sinking line and an extra reel to keep it on.)
- You don't need an extra reel for a sinking tip since you can just attach it to the floating line that you have on the reel, using the loop-to-loop connection.
- To use the sinking tip's sinking characteristics, cast it and count to ten before you strip the line. (There is more to it than that, as I have since learned, but this is what Newell told me at the time, and it worked, so I am leaving the statement in. See more detail on the subject below in the section entitled "**An Important Observation for a Newbie about Sinking Lines and Tips**".)
- Newell put a loop on a RIO Powerflex Core Sinking Tapered Leader ($13) using three nail knots. He looped the part of the sinking tip that is toward the fly. He used 12 pound test monofilament wrapped five to seven times around the base of the loop (see the figure below). He then tied it with a nail knot. He put three of these wraps and the nail knot on the base of the loop. You can see this in the figure. Note that you really need to make the knots tight. Use pliers!!

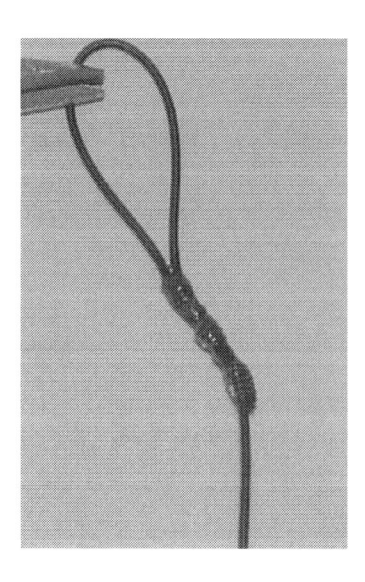

Figure 10-1 Sinking Tip Leader Loop

Sinking Line
- Being longer, and having been designed specifically for the purpose, it allows you to get further down into the water column.
- I bought a spare ROSS Cimarron reel and put my sinking line on it. I now have a reel for my floating line and one for my sinking line.
- Since this is a fly line it needs a leader, so I put on a 9 foot 3x leader (just like the one that I would put on for the floating line). I probably could have just used some 20 pound test monofilament since the tapering of a commercial leader is not really necessary in this case (I don't need to smoothly transmit the energy for a delicate presentation).

Okay now I have my sinking tip rigged up by Newell. Rather than trek back up to the Conowingo Dam, he said that I should go to Fletcher's Boat House on the Potomac River, row out to the main water channel and cast downstream. I should let out 40 to 50 feet of line and then strip it in once it settles down. When I catch a fish, strip it in and get it into the boat. He told me to try about 20 casts of the chartreuse fly, then red, then white until they bite.

If the fish is monstrous (and they can be a lot bigger than brookies or smallies), let it run with reel drag to tire it out a little bit, and then strip the line and get it onto the reel. "Getting it onto the reel" means to turn the handle of the reel until the line that you have stripped is gone onto the reel and you are tight to the fish.

Newell cautioned me not to have the rod go to more than a 45 degree angle when fighting the fish since I could break off the rod tip. He also recommended that I use shad darts as I said above, so I picked up two each of the colors chartreuse, red, white.

As you will see below, he was absolutely correct in all of his advice to me, so read what he told me again before you go after shad.

The next day, I went to Fletcher's Boat House on Canal Road where I rented a boat. In April 2005, it cost me $21.15 to rent the boat. It is now $29 as I write this a year later due to the cost of the new boats (about $3000) and the governmental fees (about $900). They supply life vests and oars. Fletcher's Boat House is open from 7AM to 7 PM, Monday through Friday. On Saturdays they open at 6 AM. By the way, they don't rent boats (by law) if the river is too high, so call the day before if you are not sure that the water level is safe to fish from a boat.

Before I tell you about my Potomac shad fishing experience, here is a valuable tip about getting to and from Fletcher's Boat House. You almost always have to **back your car down** the entrance road (at the Stone House) if you are NOT coming from the D. C. direction. **(You may be able to make a hard 180 degree left, if it's early in the morning and there is no cross traffic, but I have always backed down whenever I have gone to Fletcher's Boat House).**

By the way, I am assuming that it is before 10 AM in the morning, so Canal Road is two lanes, going one way into D. C. Since I am coming from Vienna, I go over Chain Bridge and make a right onto Canal Road. When you see the Stone House off to your right, pull over just past the road going down to the C&O canal.

Now for the shad fishing. It was great and nothing like I have ever experienced before. These fish really fight you and are big! I followed Newell's advice to the letter.

I tried a chartreuse shad dart and got bites, but they wouldn't stay on. Susanne Malone, AKA "flyfishgrl", an expert fly-fisher whom I had seen at a Trout Unlimited meeting, and who was fishing nearby suggested the white one. She even gave me one of hers. With that final piece of the puzzle in place, I caught ten Hickory shad that day, and could have caught more. The picture below shows the first of the ten. My shoe is in the picture to give an idea of its size. My shoe is 12 inches long.

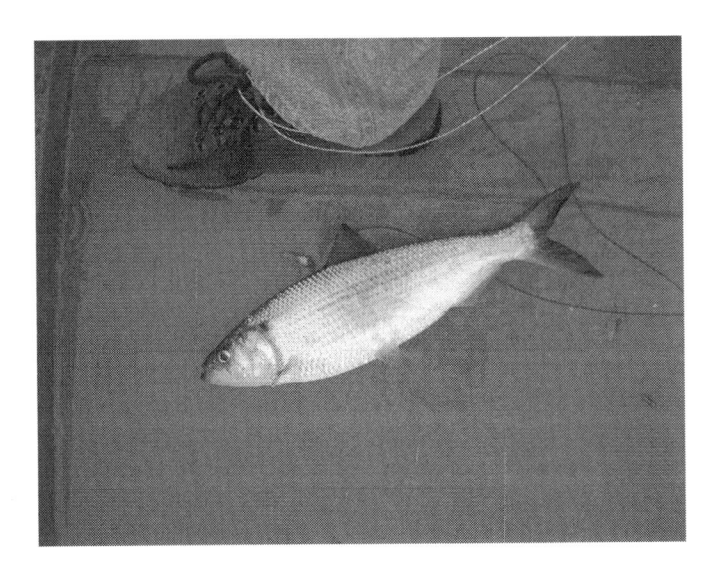

Figure 10-2 My First Shad

I caught several shad that were about 14" long (mouth to the V in the tail). I used the 7 weight Sage rod (with a ROSS Cimarron 3 reel) that I had bought at The Angler's Lie. I used my normal floating line, but put the sinking tip on it and a white shad dart on the leader, which in this case is just some 0X tippet.

By the way, the first day wasn't just luck. The next week I went to Fletcher's Boat House again, fished until noon and caught about ten white perch (see picture below), some smallmouth bass, and seven shad.

Figure 10-3 My First Perch (on a fly)

The perch were caught on a shad dart (see the picture) using an across and down retrieve. I let the sinking tip sink right after casting and then started stripping. I got a lot of fish while the line was making the turn from downstream towards me as the books tell you. Some shad were also caught that way, but a lot of the shad were caught using the trolling technique Newell suggested. I would wiggle the line out of the back of the boat to let it out and then retrieve it.

Afterwards I went to The Angler's Lie and talked to Newell about technique. This is a good thing to do in that you are fresh from fishing and any tips that are given really sink in (pardon the pun). Newell said that if I needed to, I could tire the fish by watching my line and then making my rod go in the opposite direction that the fish was going, rather than forcing it to go side to side like I had been doing. If the fish goes straight, then go either direction. For really big fish, just let the fish do what it wants to do.

He also said that I should have stripped very rapidly rather than doing the slow retrieve that I used. Throw 60 or so feet of line and then strip rapidly.

So that is my shad fishing story. It started badly, but I ended up really learning a lot and being able to test the theory of using a sinking tip to get down to where the fish are.

I leave this chapter with something that I have learned this year (one year after the Shad Fiasco that I related above). It illustrates how much of a newbie that I still am, and how far I still have to go in learning the sport of fly-fishing.

An Important Observation for a Newbie about Sinking Lines and Tips
"Now hear this!" as I heard many times in the Navy. Sinking lines and tips are made specifically to sink at a designed rate! Of course, it depends on some factors, such as, the current and whether or not the water is salty. However, if you just blindly cast out the line without COUNTING, then you are really at the mercy of luck. When Newell told me to cast out the line with the sinking tip and count to ten, he was in effect telling me to allow the fly to get down at least 56 inches (about 4.5 feet). This is because the sinking tip that he sold to me (a RIO Powerflex Core Sinking Leader) is designed to sink at a rate of 5.6 inches per second.

Suppose that I had tossed the line out and began retrieving it immediately? Then I would have gained almost nothing from the tip relative to not having it on in the first place.

It is therefore <u>very, very important</u> to COUNT after the line or tip hits the water in order to estimate how far down the fly is, BEFORE you start stripping line. By COUNTING you will get access to fish that are holding at various depths in the water. I have learned this the hard way this year (April 2006)! I have been out for shad twice and have only caught five of them (compared with about 17 last year). The major difference from last year is that I was using a full sinking line that sinks at a rate of 4.75 inches per second rather than 5.6 inches per second for the sinking tip.

This year I forgot to COUNT! I am a newbie, so what can I say. I have learned my lesson, however, and I hope that you will learn from my stupidity. In analyzing what could be going wrong this year relative to last year, I would say that last year I had gotten down to where the fish were, whereas this year I just didn't. On the second day that I was out this year, I spent three hours and caught one Hickory, while in a boat not that far away from me, a spincaster was pulling them in left and right. I am not kidding. He must have caught at least 20 shad over that time. I learned later that the fish were biting on any color of shad dart that he was throwing, so that was not a factor. (By the way, I had tried three colors during the time that I was fishing.)

What I should have done was tried different counts to get to different depths. The one shad that I caught probably just happened to be at the right depth when I luckily happened to be going by him. I'll take him, but I ain't bragging.

Learn from my mistake, COUNT!!!

11 Nymphing

In the chapter on the Mountain Trout School, I gave you my notes with comments. These notes included some on nymph fishing. Since I consider nymph fishing to be so important for newbies, I am going to devote a separate chapter to it. Some of the material will be redundant to my previous notes, but that will just serve to reinforce some information and techniques, which is a good thing.

I have read that 70 to 80 percent of a fish's diet is taken underwater. So why would you not try to catch fish this way, especially when you are getting skunked with your top water fishing? After talking with a few people on this subject, it seems that nymphing (that is, fishing with nymphs) is sort of looked down on as something akin to spincasting with a bobber. Well, I don't care what other people think; I just want to catch fish.

I have come to enjoy nymphing. In fact, is it that much different than using streamers to catch smallmouth bass? It's underwater, isn't it? I have caught a lot of bass and can't say that I have been disappointed that it wasn't on a top water fly. Don't get me wrong, I have caught many a smallie and other fish on, say, poppers; but to me the excitement is more in the catching than in where it occurred. After all, even if the fish takes a top water fly it immediately goes down. It is all a matter of taste, I guess.

Anyway, let me recommend to you that you learn to fish nymphs like the one I have used in the figure below. Go ahead and try that Adams or Comparadun or other top water fly. Pick the right size and color for the fly that will "match the hatch", sneak up on the pool, find the feeding station, make the perfect cast, and get the perfect drift with no drag. This is a lot of fun because you can see the fish take the fly and gives you a lot of satisfaction when you catch it. However, if this is not working well, try a nymph!

Figure 11-1 Gold Ribbed Bead Head Hare's Ear Nymph

Now, being a newbie at fly-fishing I can't give you all of the expert tips and techniques for nymphing, but the following is what I have learned. It works for me in that I have caught a lot of fish doing what I am going to tell you now.

First of all, logic tells me (there goes that engineer in me again) that the nymph must be somewhere near the bottom of the pool or stream bed, so make sure that you have enough weight on it to get it down there. I like bead head nymphs for this purpose.

The bead head not only provides some weight, but also adds some flash that attracts the fish. I have also read that it looks like an air bubble that is used to get the nymph to the surface, so it looks like a natural element of a real nymph.

If the nymph (using a bead head or not) does not have enough weight by itself, add some splitshot (lead or tungsten balls with a slit down their middle) six to twelve inches above the nymph. This way it will bounce along the bottom and look like it's swimming.

Now approach the water (do it as silently as you can), cast it pretty much anywhere you think that fish are located (don't let it splash onto the water really hard or it will spook the fish) and retrieve it slowly. That's about it for the way I nymph fish.

Of course, there are various nymphing techniques that you can learn (and I use them), but I don't want to confuse you at this point in your learning process if you are new to fly-fishing.

The above will get you started; however, you must realize that you will miss a fair number of fish because they spit out the nymph before you know that they are there.

In the above I am trading off simplicity for number of fish caught and relying on the fact that some fish will "hook themselves". If you want to catch more fish by nymphing (after you have gotten a taste for it using the previous technique), try the Leisenring Lift. It is easy to learn and keeps the line relatively tight to the nymph, thereby alerting you more quickly to a hit so that you can set the hook.

The nice thing about nymphing is that you don't need as much finesse as with top water fishing. I do recommend, however, that you read up on nymphing techniques, or go to the web, or take a class when you are ready to catch more fish that proper technique and more knowledge will provide. What I have told you above is good enough for now.

I am going to end this chapter with some of my observations on nymphing versus top water fishing. I give them in the following table; however, as I have said several times throughout the book, these are just my opinions. You will naturally form your own opinions as a result of talking to people and as your experience grows. Whatever works for you ---USE IT! It makes no difference what I say or any expert says, if you are catching fish and are enjoying the sport, then you have become a fly-fisher.

Table 11-1 Top Water versus Nymphing Observations

Top Water Pros
1. First and foremost, it is exciting to actually see the fish take the fly.
2. You get a lot of satisfaction from knowing that you properly imitated whatever it was that the fish are feeding on; that is, you have correctly "matched the hatch."
3. You can take pride in making the perfect cast; that is one that lands were you wanted it to land and sets the fly down with almost no noise.
4. You can know that you properly drifted the fly; that is, the fly looks just like it would if it were not attached to your leader.

Top Water Cons
1. Fish feed on top water flies only 20 to 30 percent of the time, so your chances of catching them are correspondingly smaller.
2. Your chances of catching the fish are smaller if you don't properly match the hatch.
3. Your chances of catching the fish are smaller if you don't get it to drift properly.
4. You can't put the fly into riffles or other water that will sink it because it will probably need to be dried and dressed with floatant before your next cast.

Nymphing Pros
1. First and foremost, you have more opportunity to catch more fish. This is not only because of the statistics stated before, but also because you can fish the riffles and other turbulent water in the stream. In fact, this is exactly where you want to try your nymph first, as this is where there is the most oxygen and where a lot of natural nymphs are washed into the stream.
2. When you are fishing the riffles, the noise of the rushing water helps hide your presence.
3. The nymph is naturally wet, so you don't have to dress it or worry about its floating properly.

Nymphing Cons
1. You won't see the fish take your nymph.
2. You will miss some fish by not detecting the strike (strike indicators may help).
3. You will get hung up on a rock or other underwater obstacle from time-to-time and therefore lose more flies this way, and/or have to put down the pool to get your fly back.

12 Tying Flies

I just got into tying flies this last winter. This is after about two years since taking up fly-fishing. Since I can afford the flies that I need for my fishing, fly-tying is just an educational experience for me. Also, it allows me to answer "Yes" to the question "Do you tie your own flies?" For some reason, this is the first question that someone asks you when they find out that you fly-fish. I don't know why. This chapter will give you my thoughts on getting into this aspect of the sport from a newbie point of view. It won't be a lot, but I hope that it will help.

Okay, suppose you want to start tying flies. Well, you need the equipment, the material and some recipes (fly patterns) for the flies that you want to tie. It is overwhelming and you are going to make a lot of incorrect choices, thereby costing you a lot of money that you didn't need to spend. Here are a few observations that can help you avoid this.

Based upon what I have found so far, my advice is to get the <u>CHEAPEST</u> introductory fly-tying kit that you can buy. I got one from L. L. Bean shown in the figure below for $50. I have seen the same kit at The Angler's Lie from Wapsi, whose book was included in my kit. I suspect it is the same one with L. L. Bean reselling it. The kit had everything that I needed to get started, <u>AND</u>, more importantly, it has gotten me up on the learning curve just enough to be able to ask the right questions and make some informed choices.

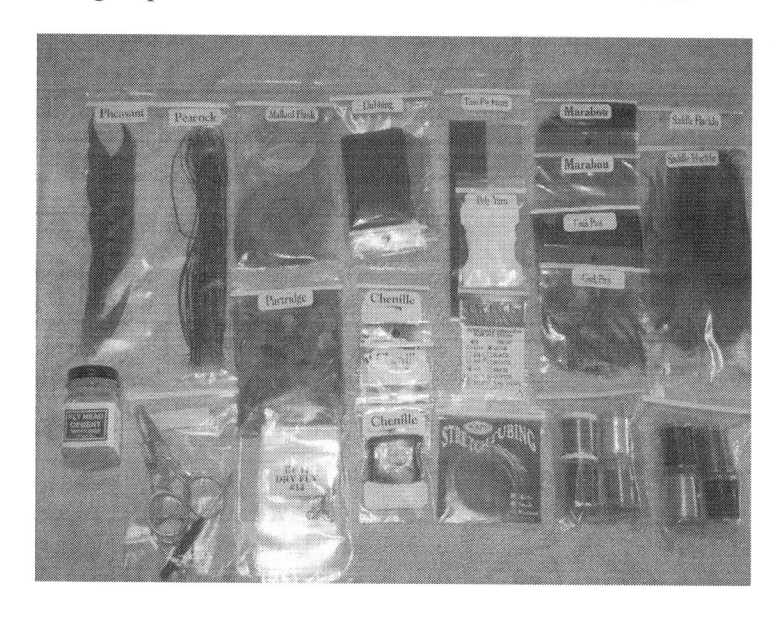

Figure 12-1 L. L. Bean Fly-tying Starter Kit

I say this because after tying some flies you learn what you like in a vise, bobbin, etc. and what you don't like, as well as become familiar with the materials, cement, tinsel, etc. that a particular fly calls for.

A good example is the vise, which is a major cost item in fly-tying. It can cost anywhere from about $8 (No kidding! I saw one on sale at Cabella's) to over $250. $250 is a lot of money to lay out at the beginning when you don't have a clue as to what you like and/or really need. The one that came with my kit is shown below.

Figure 12-2 My Cheapo Vise

It actually does the job very well. I have noted only one drawback so far, namely, that it would be a lot easier to wrap peacock herl (which is used in some flies, but is rather fragile) if I could hold the herl and the thread together while turning the hook shank, rather than vice versa. A full rotary vise would make this particular aspect of fly-tying a lot easier. See what I mean about experience? I wouldn't have known about this if I hadn't tied a fly.

Will I get a full rotary vise? I don't know yet. I need more experience, and I don't tie that many flies where a little inconvenience bothers me. I also don't need to crank out a lot of flies per hour. From what I have been told, the jaws in my cheapo vise will cease to hold flies properly after awhile. I will probably upgrade then.

As I said before, the major reason for going with the cheap vise that comes with the kit like the one I bought is that it allows me to compare it with the ones that other people have, for example, at the Trout Unlimited meetings. Before our chapter meetings, one or more of the accomplished fly tiers demonstrate how to tie a given fly and give some pointers along the way. I am able to see several vises of various designs at those sessions in actual use rather than just a picture in a catalog. Without having used a vise I wouldn't know what its features were and whether or not I would like to have those features in a vise that I might purchase later.

<u>So, what I am telling you here is to tie several flies with a starter kit, and then you will be in a much better position to make the purchases that are right for you.</u>

As a side note, one of the reasons why I do anything like fly-fishing or fly-tying in the first place is that I love to learn! In taking up fly-tying, I have opened up my life to the range of materials that are used. I want to know all about them, not just use them.

So one of the aspects of fly-tying that I have found interesting is finding out what peacock herl is. Some of it came in the kit and it is used in a lot of flies. However, I want to know why is it used? Well, it turns out that it gives a lot of flash to the fly and it changes color based upon the angle of the light falling on it, so it looks alive. Now wasn't that a lot more fun than just using it and not knowing why?

Okay, peacock herl has flash and color, but what the heck is it? In one version of the Zug Bug (a nymph imitator) pattern, the tail is peacock sword (although another pattern says you can use herl). Well, it turns out that the sword is a side feather from the bird; whereas the herl is the part of the tail just below the eye that everyone identifies with the peacock. The sword and the herl have different characteristics that fly-tiers have found make a fly more lifelike.

As I learn more and more facts about the material and better techniques for tying a fly, I will obtain more enjoyment from fly-tying. This is my goal.

I am sure that you are aware of this, but I will state it anyway; namely, that there are a ton of tutorials on the web. Some even have video with them. For example, one shows you how to whip finish a fly, which is an "advanced" way to secure the thread so that it won't come unraveled. One such website is http://www.westfly.com/. It has lots of good info on all kinds of flies. It is an excellent site!

I will end this chapter by showing you a Hare's Ear Nymph that I tied. It is shown in the figure below. Not bad if I do say so myself, and even better, I caught over 25 bluegills on it. Yes, I know that I could have thrown just about anything at them, and they would have taken it, but I'm happy. And it proves that I didn't produce a fly that is so bad that even they wouldn't think that it was food.

Figure 12-3 My Hare's Ear Nymph

13 Odds and Ends

In this section I will gather together some things that didn't easily fit into the other chapters, and/or did not have a story associated with them. These are subjects that I have wrestled with, and since I have come to some conclusions on them, I would like to pass them on to you. On each subject I will give you why I do what I do today, and some background on the path that I took in getting there.

13.1 Thoughts on Leaders

This section and the following one present my thoughts on rigging up a rod and reel, observations that I have made along the way, as well as passing on tips that others have given to me that have turned out to be quite useful.

Rigging consists of the "fly line backing" on the reel hub (arbor), which is connected to the fly line, which is connected to the leader. A leader, and I am restricting myself to leaders used with floating lines in this section (see my section on the Shad Fiasco for some discussion on sinking tips, lines and leaders for them.), is the business end of the rigging, being as invisible as it can be so as to fool the fish into thinking that the fly is all by itself. A leader has two identifiable parts, the butt or thickest section and the tippet or thinnest section. (If it is knotted, then there will be sections between the butt and the tippet.)
When you buy a new leader, it is naturally wound up in its package. Obviously there are two ways to unwind it; one starting at the tippet end and the other from the butt end. I was told by a guy at Orvis that it is best to unwind the leader from the thick end of the loop. I agree! I have done it both ways and the thin part tends to wrap on itself and tangle more easily if you unwind it from that end.
Next, there is a problem with leaders having "memory"; that is, whenever they are wrapped around anything for any length of time, they will want to stay coiled up. This could be when they first come out of the package or when they have been wrapped around the reel arbor for awhile. To get the memory out of a leader, run it back and forth around a **<u>smooth round</u>** piece of metal like a light poll or trailer hitch. Make sure it doesn't have any nicks or other sharp surfaces that can cut it. You can also use a glove (rubber or leather), or your fingers, however, your fingers can get cut or at least rubbed raw, so be careful if you use fingers to get the memory out.

Now let's talk about the subject of knotted versus unknotted leaders. The figure below shows what I mean by a knotted leader. It is just a leader made up of sections of monofilament of decreasing thickness going from the butt section (attached to the fly line) down to the tippet section (attached to the fly itself). The figure also shows a slide-on strike indicator. It has been put on during the leader construction. Doing so afterwards would be very difficult since you would have to push the indicator over the leader knots.

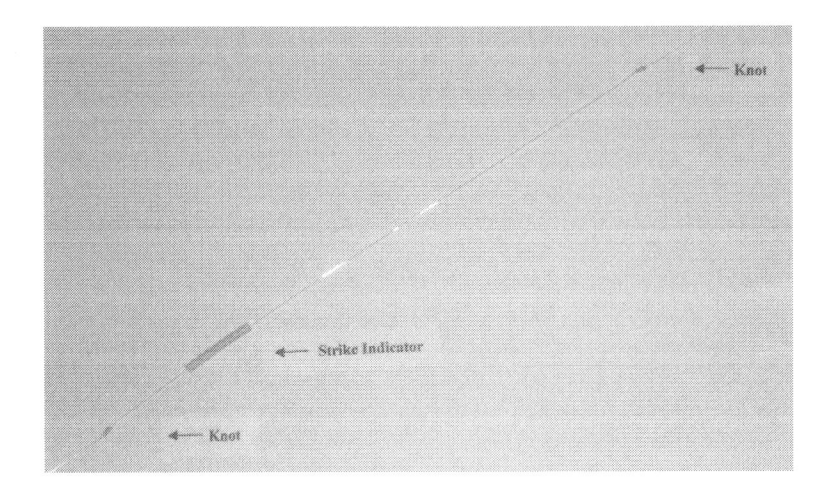

Figure 13-1 Knotted Leader Section with Strike Indicator

I have gone through many iterations before coming to the conclusions that I am about to give you. I started off with unknotted leaders for my original outfit and then I was introduced to knotted leaders when I bought my 3 weight outfit. The pros and cons of each seemed clear at each point in time; however, experience, as always, has led me to what works best for me now. This is not to say that I won't change my mind later; but here are my conclusions on the subject, and more importantly, why I believe the way I do.

The primary thing that I don't like about knotted leaders is that they are a pain to deal with when most of the leader is in the guides, for example, for close-in fishing on mountain streams. Also they are hard to straighten out since you can't just pull them through your fingers in one pass.

I used a knotted leader for my mountain trout fishing in 2004 and have since switched to an unknotted one. I don't see any difference in my results so far. What I would guess is that at my level of expertise, the supposedly extra finesse available with a knotted leader is not my biggest fishing technique problem. When I asked Newell at The Angler's Lie about the subject, he said that he does not use knotted leaders. Harry Murray, on the other hand, swears by them.

I am going with unknotted leaders for now until I have a good reason to switch to the knotted ones. If you have to use knotted leaders, however, the key to using them is to NOT have them in the guides. In other words, reel in enough line while fishing to not have them there, but with enough leader out to do your fishing. In mountain trout fishing, you are close anyway and so you don't really cast far. You essentially pull out enough line and flip it to the spot that you want to fish. The leader is mostly out of the guides and should not cause a problem in that respect.

The table below summarizes the above thoughts on knotted versus unknotted leaders.

Table 13-1 Knotted versus Unknotted Leaders Pros and Cons

Knotted Leader Pros
- You can make them delicate (using lots of sections) and fine tune them to your situation.
- You can see when your tippet is in need of replacement easily (**this is NOT an advantage**, however, when using the looped system that I describe in the section on knots and loops for rigging since you know where the tippet starts for both knotted and knotless leaders).
- You can cut off the thinnest part of the leader if you want a heavier tippet (although I can easily change the leader if I am using the looped system). It is in effect changing to a heavier leader.

Knotted Leader Cons
- You can pick up debris like algae on the knots.
- They won't go through the guides as easily as tapered leaders due to the knots.
- It is harder to put slide-on indicators due to the knots.

Tapered (Unknotted) Leader Pros
- They go through the guides easily due to no knots to hang up on them. Note that the butt/tippet loop-to-loop connection that is at the very end of the leader should never be in the guides, so it is not a hang-up problem like the knots in the knotted leader.
- You can easily put on "slide-on" strike indicators (use part of a tooth pick to lock them in place).

Tapered (Unknotted) Leader Cons
- Supposedly not as much finesse possible. (This may be true, but I haven't seen any difference so far.)

13.2 Knots and Loops for Rigging

Now I am going to tell you about what knots I use for the various connections that are needed in rigging up your rod and reel. As I said above, this starts with the fly line backing-to-the reel arbor (its hub) connection and ends with the tippet-to the-fly connection.

There are several knots that can be employed. I am not going to list all of the alternatives precisely because too many alternatives just confuse the issue. I am simply going to tell you what I use. It works for me, so you can use them for now. Later you can try different ones as you are more comfortable with the subject and are curious about what the other knots are.

I hope that I am not going to confuse you by all of the words that it takes to describe the knots and loops. Unfortunately, it is much easier to show someone rather than to write down the instructions. Hopefully you will get the idea and be able to get yourself rigged up properly. If you are still perplexed, the folks at your local fly shop will be happy to show you how to do it. Come to think of it, that is probably the best way to learn this subject, but it is also nice to have it written down somewhere. What I do is write my own notes in the margins of my books in places where the words are a little confusing to me.

Table 13-2 Rod/Reel Connections

1. **Backing to arbor (hub) of the reel**: Arbor knot

2. **Backing to Fly line's Backing End**: Albright knot (glued)

3. **Fly Line's Leader End**:
   a. Use a nail knot to connect a short piece (about six inches) of 15-20 pound test monofilament (0X tippet is fine) to the fly line. Apply some glue that won't dissolve in water (obviously).

   By the way, I think that a needle knot is too much trouble, but if you want to use it, note the following. The needle is NOT used to thread the leader. Rather it is used to make the hole so that a leader can be threaded through the hole. Note also that you can heat the needle after it is through the end of the fly line to set the hole. The advantage of the needle knot is that it lets the monofilament come out of the center of the fly line rather than off to the side like the nail knot, thereby going through the guides more easily. Applying Pliobond (see the next bullet) solves this problem with the nail knot, so I use the nail knot.

   b. Apply Pliobond if you desired. It's not required for knot strength, but rather is used so that the connection pulls through the rod guides smoothly. Pliobond is a thick glue-like material that you can buy at most fly shops, a lot of hardware stores or online.

   c. Use a perfection or triple surgeon's loop on the other end of the monofilament and Pliobond the knot part of the loop. (Note that you can use a small piece of the butt section of an old leader instead of the monofilament mentioned above if you have some lying around. It doesn't matter that the butt part of the tapered leader is tapered [if it is], since you are not using much of it and it doesn't affect the rest of the leader.

d. We now have a loop with which to connect the leader to the fly line.

From here on, I use loop-to-loop connections for everything else (except for the fly itself, of course)

4. **Leader Butt End**:
    a. Leaders from manufacturers often have a loop on the butt end of the leader (for example, RIO uses a perfection loop). If it doesn't have a loop, then put one on using a perfection or triple surgeon's loop.

    b. Pliobond the knot part of the loop again if you desire.

5. **Leader Tippet End**:

Here is something that I do that I think is very useful, but have not seen anywhere else so far in my travels or reading.

Every time that you tie a fly to the tippet, you naturally lose tippet. With a tapered leader it is hard to know where to apply more tippet. Also multiple knots will eventually require you to replace the whole leader itself.

I get around this problem by taking a **new** leader and measuring up about 30 inches from the tippet end (where the fly is attached). I cut it there, and then put a triple surgeon's loop on both parts of the tippet where I made the cut. This gives me a loop-to-loop connection. I then can easily see when I have to change tippet and I simply take off the old tippet (now shorter due to multiple ties of the flies that you have fished with), put a loop on the new tippet, and connect it to the butt section's loop.

I should tell you that I sometimes have to use a safety pin (maybe two) to disconnect the loops if they are very tight and won't come undone easily. I always keep two safety pins on my vest on the foam where I put the flies that I have used.

Now that we have all of our loops, here is how to connect any two of them. Put the **loop** on the line or leader that eventually goes back to the reel (I will call this the "reel end") through the **loop** that eventually goes forward to the fly (I will call this the "fly end"). Now pass the **free end of the line** that is attached to the "fly end" loop through the "reel end" **loop** and pull the loops tight. They should lie down like a square knot. It will be obvious to you if you have done it incorrectly. It is a good idea to check that it looks like a square knot **BEFORE** you tighten the connection.

6. **Tippet to Fly**: 16-20 knot (discussed below)

First a little discussion. The main reason that I can see for different knot choices, besides personal preference, is how well the knot holds. Its strength depends on its design, of course, but also on the thickness and material of the two lines that it is connecting.

To make my point, here is a **ridiculous example**. Suppose I wanted to connect a 7 weight line to the tippet end of a leader. The problem that I run into is the tremendous difference in diameters of the two lines (fly line and tippet). There are knots that can do the job; however, there are knots that I definitely would not want to use. The lighter line has a tendency to slide right past the thicker fly line in certain knots making the knot fail when tension is applied to it. So they are not appropriate for this situation.

Another reason that one knot is used over another is how easy it is to tie given the thickness and material of the line. To illustrate this point, I like the triple surgeon's loop a lot. It is simple in design and strong. However, one time I tried to use it for putting a loop on the end of my 7 weight line and found that it was way too bulky. When I had done the same thing on my 3 weight line, it worked well. The solution for the 7 weight line was to nail-knot a piece of monofilament line to the fly line, and then put the loop in the monofilament.

In the table above I used the term "fly line backing." If you are a real newbie then you may not know what fly line backing is. So before I continue, let me tell you that backing is used to fill out the arbor with cheaper line than a fly line, and also to give you a "heads up" when you have run out of fly line when a fish runs.

They sell large arbor reels to minimize the amount of backing that is needed, but backing is cheap, so I haven't bought one of those large arbor reels yet. Oh yes, the backing also minimizes the coiling tightness that the fly line has when it wraps around the arbor. This reduces the memory effect due to this problem, especially when a reel with fly line is stored over the winter.

So for the fly line backing to the reel, I use an arbor knot. It is simple and not too bulky. For the backing to the fly line I use a triple surgeon's knot. It lays flat.

13.3 The 16-20 Knot

I previously used the uni-knot described later for all my tippet-to-fly connections; however, I saw the 16-20 knot on one of my travels on the web and fell in love with it. Supposedly it is stronger than the Improved Clinch Knot. You can do a search of the web to see several examples of how to tie it; however, I have found that the way I do it makes it easier for me. It is a great knot.

Here is Dave's way of tying the 16-20 knot. I am left-handed, so reverse the instructions if you are right-handed.

13 Odds and Ends

- Hold the hook in your left hand.
- Thread the tag end of the tippet through the eye (**from the bottom up**) and around your **middle** finger (This is an important part of making the knot easy to tie because you can pull on both sides of the line while doing the wraps.)
- With your **right** hand, pass the line that is going out of the eye (the tag end of the tippet) **in back** of the line that is going into the eye (the part of the tippet connected to the butt of the leader), and then **pinch** the lines together with the **thumb** and **first finger** of your right hand. (Note: Passing the tag in back of the line - **NOT IN FRONT** - is important!!!)
- The amount of tippet that you have available for the knot is measured by having the tag end's tip approximately at the knuckle of your right hand where the finger connects to the hand itself (the third knuckle from the finger tip). This is not important now, just use a lot of tippet or whatever line you are practicing with. Later you can minimize the tippet loss by the above measurement technique.
- Grab the tag end of the tippet between the thumb and first finger of your left hand and make **five wraps** using the second finger of your right hand to do the wrapping.
- Grab the **tag** end of the tippet again and pinch the wraps with the thumb and first finger of your right hand while **slipping** the middle finger of your left hand out of its position next to the hook eye.
- **Expose** the loop that was under your right hand.
- Pass the tag end of the tippet through the loop.
- **Wet** the knot with saliva and tighten it **a little** by pulling on the **tag**, but **not all the way**.
- Pull the knot down to the eye.
- **Snug** the wraps down to the eye with the fingernails of your left hand (this is also a key part of tying the knot).
- Pull on the leader part of the tippet and the hook to secure the knot.
- You should feel a pop. (Oftentimes I don't, however.) This is a sign that the knot was done correctly.
- Test the knot for strength.

The pictures below show three key stages in the tying of the 16-20 knot. The first one (Part 1) shows how you let the tag end of the tippet go **behind** the rest of the leader. The second one (Part 2) shows the knot after the wraps have been done before putting the tag end of the tippet through the loop. The last one (Part 3) shows the knot just before it has been tightened (with the tag end having been put through the loop). Note that the paper clip is substituting for the hook.

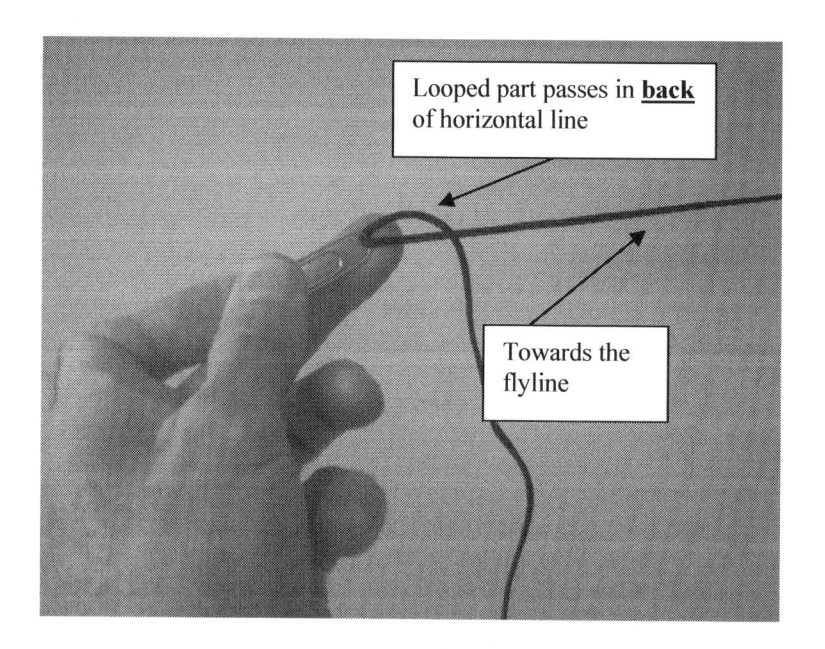

Figure 13-2 Forming the 16-20 Knot (Part 1)

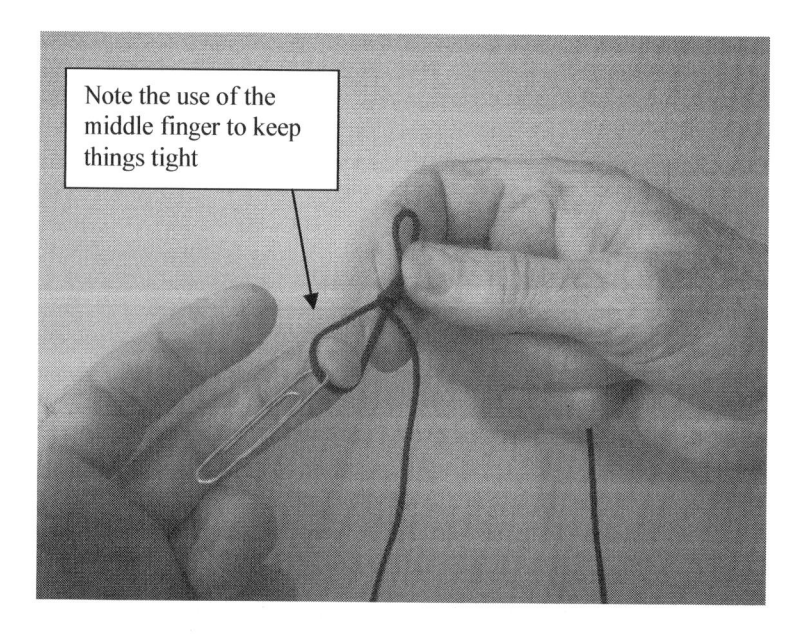

Figure 13-3 Forming the 16-20 Knot (Part 2)

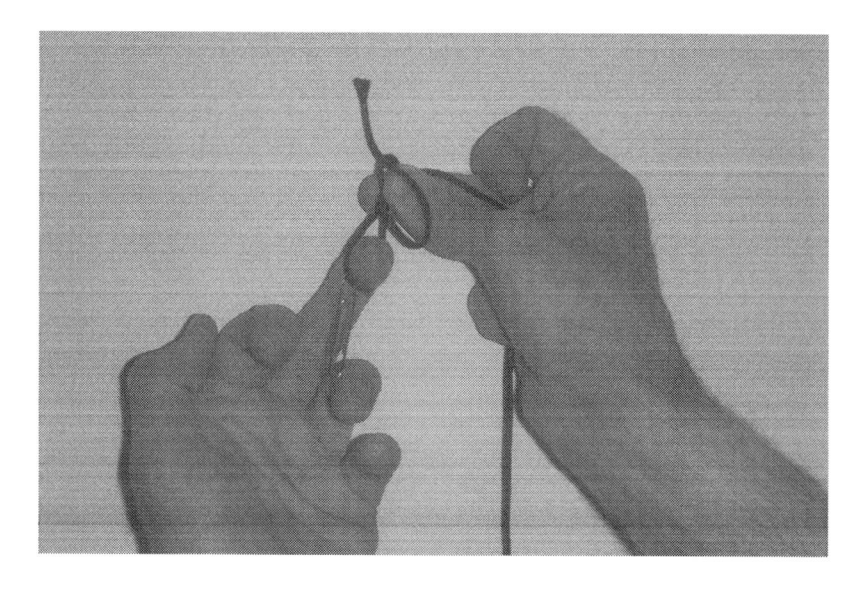

Figure 13-4 Forming the 16-20 Knot (Part 3)

13.4 The Uni-knot (Duncan Loop)

The uni-knot is the one that I used the most for tying my flies to the tippet before I switched to the 16-20 knot. The uni-knot is also called the Duncan Loop. The reason that I prefer this knot over the Improved Clinch Knot, which by the way I used for years in my spincasting life, is because I find that the uni-knot is easier for me to tie and there is only one loop to deal with. Also, from an engineering standpoint, the multiple wraps around itself vastly reduce the chance that the tag end will slip through and start an unraveling process.

I am not going to tell you how to tie the uni-knot here. Go on the web, for example, "http://www.flyanglersonline.com/" for that, or see any good fishing book. However, I will point out two things that I like about the uni-knot.

1. You never have to move the hand in which you are holding the fly until you are ready to tighten the knot. In the Improved Clinch, you have to expose the eye of the hook to get to that loop, and have to move your hand to do it. At least, I have to do it this way; maybe others don't have to.

2. There is only one loop to deal with in the uni-knot. In the Improved Clinch there are two loops, one at the hook eye and the other formed by the tippet going from the wrapped section of the knot to the hook eye. I have trouble sometimes getting the tippet's tag end through hook eye loop, either because it is closed too much or I can't get to it broadside to me like I would prefer. The eye loop seems to end up edge on, making

it hard to get the tag end of the tippet through it. In the uni-knot, the loop that you are putting the wraps through is always broadside to you.

So I prefer the 16-20 knot over the uni-knot, and the uni-knot over the Improved Clinch. Using any knot is just a personal preference. The Improved Clinch may work for you. If it does USE IT! It is a good knot and I have never lost a fish by having it fail. The extra loop in it makes it very reliable.

Before leaving the uni-knot, here is a trick that makes forming the loop of the uni-knot easier. Put the tippet through the hook eye as the normal first step of tying this knot. Then, while you are holding it (and the tippet that is going through it), **wrap** the tag end around your finger tip to form the loop. Bring the tag up between your finger and thumb (which is squeezing the hook eye) and hold it securely between them. Let the loop itself slip off your finger. You now have the loop that you need! The figures below illustrate what I have said. The first one shows how I measure the amount of tag end that I need, which is nice in that you lose the same amount of tippet with each tie rather than a variable amount. Note that the paper clip is substituting for the fly.

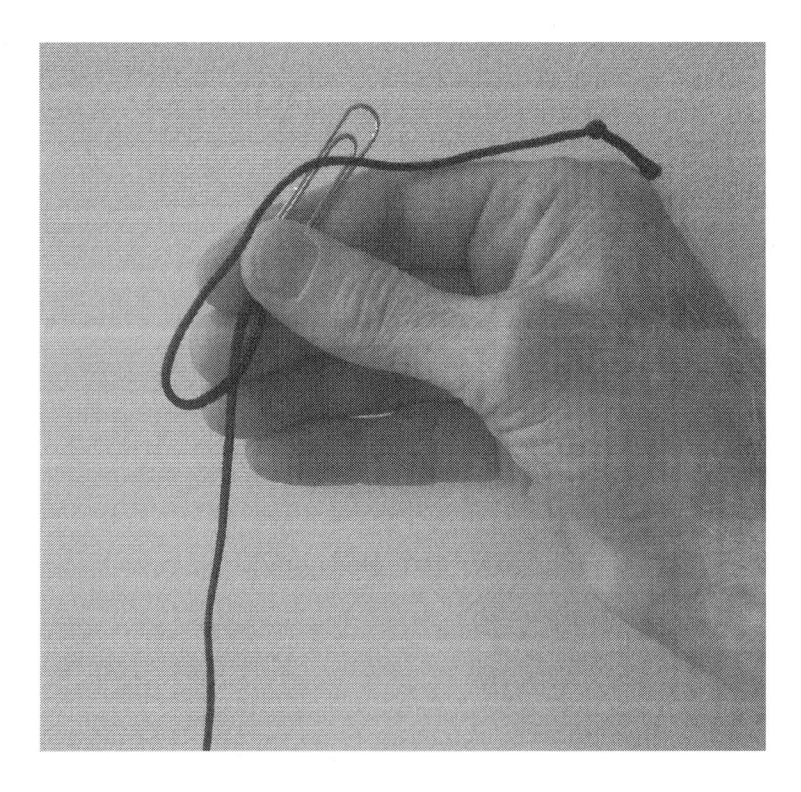

Figure 13-5 Forming the Uni-knot Loop (Part 1)

13 ODDS AND ENDS

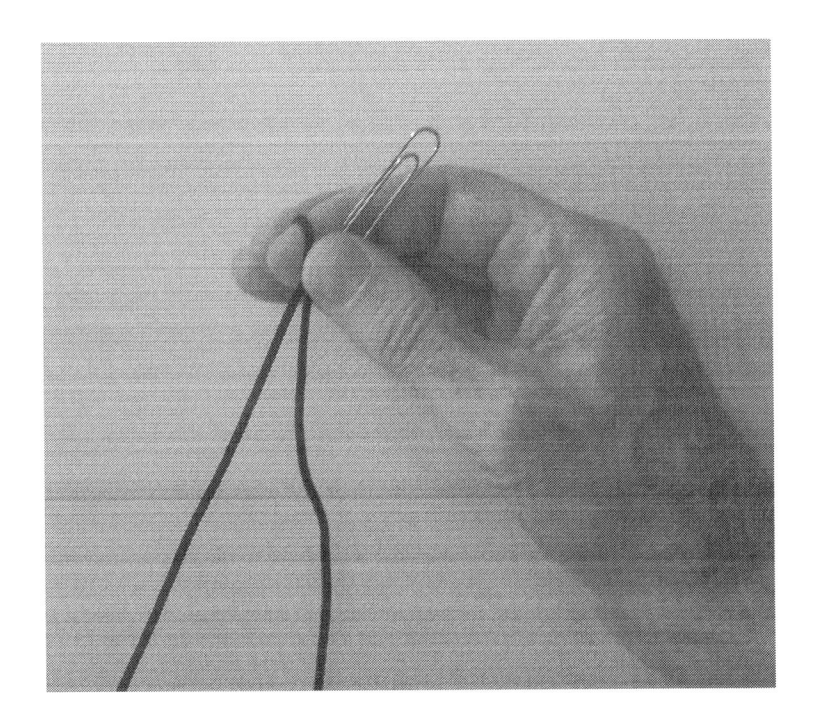

Figure 13-6 Forming the Uni-knot Loop (Part 2)

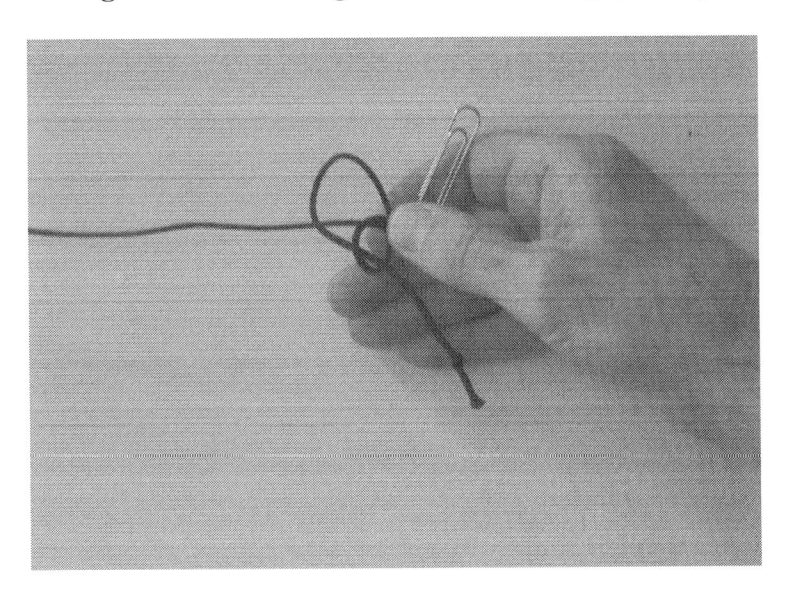

Figure 13-7 Forming the Uni-knot Loop (Part 3)

By the way, the only trouble that I have had tying the uni-knot is when the loop slips out of my fingers too soon. I have to concentrate on holding it tightly. I don't have problems then.

13.5 Casting

I put this chapter in the book because I have accumulated some tips from people that I have talked to, and because I have learned a few things myself. I also felt that any book on the subject of fly-fishing, even as rudimentary as this one, should at least talk about the basic casting technique.
I am by no means anywhere near a proficient caster. However, what I am going to write here works for me and gets the fly pretty near where I want it to be. I **really, really, recommend** that you take some casting instruction and then practice a little before going out to the place where you are going to fish. It would be very frustrating to keep hitting the trees or getting tangled up just because you had no idea how to cast. Heck, even get a video if that will do the job. Remember, however, that you don't have to be an "expert" caster to have an awful lot of fun.
Fly casting is mainly timing and keeping the tip of the fly line on a level path above your head (NOT in an arch!!!). To help you do this, try not to break your wrist (not in the broken bone sense, but in the keeping it rigid sense) when casting.
Here is the basic cast. Usually an open field is where the cast is first learned, but if you have a pond or lake nearby with a lot of open space all around where you are going to cast, that is even better. For the discussion below, I will assume that you are casting in an open field without any obstacles near you.
In the following sequence I will refer to the hand that is holding the rod as the "rod hand" and the other hand as the "line hand." This way I won't have to specialize the sequence for left-handed and right-handed persons.
I am assuming that you have your rod rigged up with fly line. If you have leader on it that is okay, but it is not really necessary for this exercise since the fly line is what gets the fly to the place where the fish is located.

- Holding the rod in your "rod hand", pull out about 20 feet of fly line from the end of the rod and lay it straight out on the ground in front of you.
- Point the rod tip down near the ground and walk back until there is NO slack in the fly line. This will allow the line to "load" (that is, bend) the rod better when you pick it up on the backcast (the part of the cast going from "in front of you" to "in back of you").
- Hold the fly line going from the reel to the rod guide nearest the reel (the stripping guide) in your "line hand".
- **Slowly** raise the rod, increasing its speed (that is, accelerating it) until the rod is just beyond the vertical position. By vertical I mean directly over the top of your head, and by "just beyond" I mean about 5 minutes back from noon if noon on a clock corresponded to the vertical position.

The rod is now slightly in back of you. By the way, a lot of people say that you should go back even further, but I have found that you will naturally do that anyway, and one of the problems that people have with casting is going back too far. For this reason, I will stop you just beyond the vertical position.

13 Odds and Ends

- I will note here that you should try to do all of the cast with only your arms, that is, do very little wrist movement. Your "line hand" should move in unison with your "rod hand."
- Stop **abruptly** at the just beyond vertical position.
- **Hesitate** a few seconds to let the line straighten out (it is a very good idea to look over your shoulder and see that the line is doing so).
- **Slowly** accelerate forward, basically repeating what you did on the back cast.
- Stop **abruptly** when your rod is about at a 45 degree angle in front of you. You don't want to have the fly line hit the ground (which will be the water when you do it for real). This will splash the water and scare the fish.
- Not hitting the ground/water also allows you to do various tricks like wiggling the rod tip when you stop. Wiggling puts some slack in the leader and gives you some nice dead drift properties when the fly hits the water.
- After the line has straightened out, slowly lower the rod to the ground. I don't mean take all day, just don't slap it down.

That is the basic cast; however, here are some things that I have learned that are important.

- The key is slow acceleration and an abrupt stop to get a snap that straightens out the line. It also loads (bends) the rod, which stores energy for the next part of the cast.
- Don't wind up when starting the forward cast. If the cast is done correctly, it will be nice and smooth, and will take very little effort.
- Use <u>very little</u> wrist action. Your wrists should be almost locked. In fact there are devices that they sell that will lock your wrist for those of you who have a lot of problems in that respect.
- Your arm should be just beyond vertical at the point where you stop your backcast, with the wrist bent slightly back.
- When the cast is finished, the line coming out of the reel is held under the first finger of "rod hand", with the "line hand" holding the line going into the stripping guide. This gets you ready for the fish strike.
- **<u>A good mantra for timing the cast is "I am CASTing" or anything that sounds like it.</u>** That is, while picking up the line you say "I am," then pause to let the line straighten out. During the forward cast say "CASTing," and pause to let the line straighten out.
- By the way, when you actually get to casting for real, put the rod tip near water (not in it) before starting the cast and swish it back and forth to let out some line. Do a roll cast, discussed below, to straighten it out. Then do your regular cast.

I will end this section with two comments related to casting that have come in handy.

- I have found that using a light rod and line when trying to cast a large (heavy) fly, like a #8 leadeyed hellgrammite, will make the casting a lot harder. The problem is that the

line is too light and leader is too flexible to throw the fly. With a heavier fly line and leader this is not a problem, however, you need a heavier rod to handle the heavier line.
- For bass and shad, a 7 weight fly line with a 2x leader is good. I was using a 5 weight rod with a 4 weight line and a 4x leader on a lead eyed hellgrammite and it didn't work very well, especially on long casts. You <u>can</u> cast it, but it will flop around all over the place and you will have no control over it.
- A "roll cast" is used to straighten line and to throw the fly when there are obstructions in back of you. **It is an extremely important cast.** You must learn to do it correctly (it isn't hard). Here is what they told me at the L. L. Bean School.
    - Form a backwards "D" with the line coming out of the water below your knees, looping around in back of you and ending up at the reel at your ear level (like you were talking on a cell phone).
    - Slowly accelerate and then flick it.
    - If there is a wind problem, then tilt the rod to the left or right (depending on the wind direction at the time) before you do the roll cast.

This should get you started. Go to the web to see videos and pictures for more detail.

13.6 Fishing Trip List

On at least one outing I forgot one or two items. One time it was my rod, so I highly recommend a checklist for the things that you want to have with you. I also highly recommend that you pack all your fishing gear in some bag or such, so that you can just pick it up and go without worrying about having left anything. Use a checklist to do the packing.

To help you in creating your own checklist, you can start with the one that I give below, which works for me, but then add or subtract items that apply for your needs. For example, I don't fish lakes yet, so I haven't included a float tube and flippers or a pontoon boat. If you fish lakes, then add the items that are needed for that.

Table 13-3 Dave's Fishing Checklist

On-Stream Items
- **Licenses:** Also, know the fishing regulations.
- **Rods and reels:** The reels should be ready to go. I always put on any leaders that are required. I also put on new tippet if it is needed since it is a lot easier to do at home. I clean up everything after each trip, dry them and put them in a duffle bag. The only things I need to do before leaving are to fill my water bottle and make my sandwich. I even have a note for that on my bag so I won't forget.
- **Fishing vest with the items below**

13 Odds and Ends

- **Flyboxes:** I have two flyboxes, one for streamer type fishing (my "B" or Bass box) and one for non-streamer type fishing (my "T" or Trout box). This way I don't have monster wooly buggers mixed in with tiny nymphs.
- **Split shot:** I have switched to tungsten shot since it is better for the environment than lead.
- **Strike Putty:** If I feel that I need it, I roll up a little bit of it into a tiny football shape and put it on the leader.
- **Thermometer:** I like to measure the water temperature since this is one of the most important factors in determining whether or not fish are going to be active or not.
- **pH Kit:** This is my personal thing so obviously you don't need it if you are not so inclined. I bought one that is used for aquariums at Wal-Mart for about $15.
- **Safety pins:** I have found these very useful for untying knots and loops, and for clearing out hook eyes.
- **Zingers:** These are handy for keeping things out of the way, but ready to use. I have zingers for my nippers and hemostats.
- **Floatant:** I use the paste type, but any that works for you is just fine.
- **Hook Sharpener:** I have tried three types of hook sharpeners, namely, a small file, a small grinding stone, and a sharpening stick that has a V groove in it. I use the latter one since the groove makes hook points a lot easier to sharpen, especially the smaller hooks.
- **Leaders:** You may have to replace the whole leader rather than just the tippet once in awhile, for example, if it gets hopelessly tangled. However, with the loop system I seldom have to change the leader itself since the loop shows me when I need new tippet. I never get too far up on the butt section of the leader so that I have to replace the whole thing just because I have tied a lot of flies onto my tippet.
- **Tippet Material:** Make sure that you are not down to the end of the spool or you could run out on-stream.
- **Hemostats:** These are absolutely essential for crimping hook barbs and more importantly, getting hooks out of fish. By the way, if a hook is too deep into a fish so that it will hurt it by extracting the hook, then cut off the tippet as far down into the fish's mouth as you can. Then release the fish. The hook will eventually dissolve.
- **Nippers:** For clipping off the tags of the tippets after attaching the fly to the it. Mine also has a pointed part to clear out hook eyes and such, as well as a hook sharpener that I can use in a pinch if I lose my main one.
- **Food:** I usually make a sandwich and have a granola bar plus quick sugar items, such as, tootsie rolls. I put these in the highest pocket that I have in case I fall down. I also put them in a Ziploc bag for this reason.
- **Safety Items:** Loud whistle, snakebite kit (I was given the "Survival Kit in a Sardine Can" as a gift and it contains a lot of good stuff.

- o **Insect repellent:** I have tried the clothing that supposedly has it built into it, but it doesn't seem to work for me or my wife.
- o **Sunblock:** I am pretty much covered most of the time, so I don't need much. A couple of times I put a handkerchief over the back of my neck to keep the sun off. I now have a hat that has a flap on it that can do the same thing if I need it. When I am not using it, it folds up underneath.
- o **Scissors:** These are always handy to have.
- o **Micro Flashlight:** I don't fish at night or dusk right now, but you never know. This one is so light and small that I carry it just for insurance.
- o **Extra Glasses and Clip-on Sunglasses:** If I lost my glasses I would be in trouble. I have always kept my old prescription glasses when I have received new ones, so I use the old ones as my backup.
- **Hat:** As I mentioned above, I have one with a flap on the back that keeps the sun off the back of my neck.
- **Sunglasses:** Always get the polarized ones so you can see the fish better. Make sure that they are light, since you will be wearing them a long time and they will get heavy.
- **Water:** I carry a water bottle. I use it for drink and for wash-up. I have tried a Camelpack, but have found that the water bottle is sufficient for me.
- **Boots and Waders** (if required).
- **Wading stick:** You also want to have something to attach it to your belt. I use a small bungee. A wading stick is a **<u>must-have</u>** item since you will fall down many times! Guaranteed! But, hey, that is part of the fun, at least for me.
- **Gloves:** I have just bought some gloves with no fingers beyond the knuckles. I really like them. They not only protect my hands, but also I can grip the fish with a lot less pressure.
- **Fish Net:** Get the lightest one that you can get within your budget constraints. I don't take a net for brook trout or bluegill fishing. When I take it for my bass or shad fishing, I carry it on a coiled plastic coated cord that has a magnetic retainer so that I can just pull it off my back when I need it. Very handy!
- **Eye glass retainers:** I have them attached to my sunglasses, which I wear over my regular glasses, so I don't have to worry about my regular glasses falling off.
- **Magnifying glasses:** I have some flipdowns attached to the brim of my fishing hat. I need these for tying flies onto the tippets. They are also good for examining nymphs and other critters, tying flies, as well as removing splinters at home.
- **Cell phone:** If there is coverage, a cell phone can come in handy in an emergency; however, put it in a waterproof container. It depends on where I am fishing as to whether or not I carry it on-stream with me.
- **Camera:** Put it in a waterproof container if you choose to bring a camera. There are cameras that are designed to be water resistant, but they are more expensive.

Non On-Stream Items
These items are helpful to have in the car or your duffle bag.
- **Maps**
- **Potomac Appalachian Trail Club hiking maps**
- **Virginia Atlas & Gazetteer by DeLORME**
- **Extra rod** (keep in the car just in case you forget, lose or break your primary rod)
- **Change of clothes and shoes**
- **Extra hat**
- **Books** and other sources of information that you might need. For example, I carry an insect guide.
- **Jug of water for wash-up**
- **Towel/Paper Towels**

13.7 Trout Stuff

Here are some very useful notes that I took from a Trout Unlimited meeting on March 2, 2006. The featured speaker was Tom Brtalik (tomsflyfishing.com), whom I had heard before, and who is a wealth of information. He told us a lot of facts about trout among other things, but I would like to repeat here just the ones that I think a newbie might want to be aware of.

Trout Requirements in Order of Importance
- The optimum water temperature for a trout is about 56 to 61 degrees. Outside of this range the trout will be harder to catch. For instance at lower temperatures, their metabolism is lower and they will not need as much food (hence less likely to take your fly). At the higher temperatures, a fish will be lethargic; so in summer, for example, you need to go in the morning or evening, or find places during the heat of the day where the water temperature is cooler, such as, deep pools and shady spots.

- The pH of the water should be between 6 and 8 with the higher reading the better. If the water is too acidic, all stream life dies. According to the Virginia Department of Game and Inland Fisheries (VDGIF), at a pH of about 5.5, frogs, crayfish and mayflies die. At 4.5, brook trout die. At 3 all fish die. As a point of reference, battery acid has a pH of 1. In comparison, baking soda and seawater have a pH of 8.5, whereas lye has a pH of 13. The rain that we get in Virginia has a pH of 4.6 (per the VDGIF although I have measured it to be considerably higher, albeit still on the acid side), so unless there is lime added to the stream or something else is present to neutralize the acid, the fish will be stressed and/or die. Obviously, if the insects die, so will the fish for lack of food.

Alkaline streams have more food and are usually spring fed, and so are very healthy.

By the way, technically pH is the negative logarithm of the hydrogen ion (H+) concentration in the water and is inversely related to the amount of the hydrogen ions in the water. Lower pH waters have more hydrogen ions and are more acidic than higher pH waters. A pH of 7 is neutral and has equal amounts of hydrogen ions (H+) and hydroxide ions (OH-). (Sorry about that, but it was the engineer in me coming out again.)

Beginning in 2006, I started measuring not only the water temperature when I go fishing, but also the pH. I got a kit from Wal-Mart for $10 in the aquarium department. So far I have taken two readings on the Hughes River and they have both been 6.8. The Potomac a little downstream from Chain Bridge read 7.2.

- All of us need oxygen to live and so does a fish. This is why turbulent water is important to fish because it oxygenates the water. You will find fish near places like this, so either fish using a nymph directly in the turbulence (riffle, etc.) or a dry fly in the seam between the turbulence and the calm water next to it. This is also part of the reason why the old saying "Foam is Home" is true.

- Fish need food, so fish spots where flies, nymphs, ants, etc. are most likely to be.

- A fish is a couch potato as much as we are in that it will minimize its energy. This is why it settles into places that block the current, like rocks and eddies.

- A fish needs protection from predators, so look for cover and structure that can provide it. If there is not a lot of cover, the fish will be spooky. Something that I have learned of late is that most of the time you will not see the structure that determines where the fish lie because it is below the surface. So throw your fly into various parts of a pool, just in case.

- Remember how fish see. They are looking up and therefore have a cone of vision. They see a cone, but the rest of the water is like a mirror. So if something drops in or floats by (like a leaf), they can see it. Turbulent water breaks up the cone of vision.

- Remember how fish hear. They have a lateral line (meaning along the side of the fish) audio sensor and an inner ear.

- Remembering how fish see and hear, it is logical to use stealth when approaching them. Don't move rapidly; move like a heron, that is, move one foot, stop, then move the other foot, stop, repeat. Note that water turbulence masks noises. This makes fishing easier due to the way fish see and hear.

- Most of the time it doesn't matter what pattern you use since the most important factors are approach and presentation.

14 References

Here are some resources that I have found to be useful. Of course the best resource is to talk to someone more knowledgeable than you are, so get to know someone at your local fly shop or join some fly-fishing group. As I've said before, I have been very pleased with my experience at our local chapter of Trout Unlimited, but other organizations can provide the interaction that you need. Get involved to whatever extent that you can.

The next best source is the web. Just type in what you want to know (I use Google) and it will usually appear. I keep a large loose leaf binder of my printouts.

Another great resource, which is free if you pick it up at a fly shop or elsewhere, is "Fly-fishing Guide." It is a monthly magazine put out by the Mid Atlantic Fly-fishing Guide in Montoursville, Pennsylvania. It is a good source for fishing and tying tips, and for keeping you pumped up to fish. I look forward to it every month.

Other than these sources, I have used the following so far in my learning.

1. Fly-fishing for Beginners by Chris Hansen, Creative Publishing International, Inc., 2003.
2. The Fly Fisherman's Bible by Jim Bashline, Broadway Books, 1993.
3. L. L. Bean Fly-Fishing handbook by Dave Whitlock, L. L. Bean, Inc. 1996.
4. The Orvis fly-Fishing Guide by Tom Rosenbauer, The Orvis Company, 1984.
5. Trout Fishing in the Shenandoah National Park by Harry W. Murray, Shenandoah Publishing Company, 1989.
6. Nymphing, A Basic Guide to Identifying, Tying, and Fishing Artificial Nymphs, Gary A. Borger, Stackpole Books, 1979
7. Trout Stream Insects by Dick Pobst, The Lyons Press, 1990.
8. The Orvis Fly-Tying Manual by Tom Rosenbauer, The Lyons Press, 2000
9. Wapsi Fly Tying Handbook, This came with my fly-tying kit.
10. Virginia Wildlife, Department of Game and Inland Fisheries, monthly by subscription.

15 Appendix A
Places to Fish and Some Fish Stories

Before I get to specific fishing spots, I want to recommend two "Must Have" items for general fishing in Virginia. The first is a topographic map like the one in the "Virginia Atlas & Gazetteer" by DeLORME. The second is really important if you are fishing the Shenandoah National Park. These are the set of maps put out by the Potomac Appalachian Trail Club, Inc. These maps give a lot of detail on the areas that we usually fish along with some parking locations. They are about $6 per map and well worth it.

Now let's get to various places that I have fished, and a few that I have heard of, but have not fished yet. I found most of them by means of the Trout Unlimited Fish With A Member (FWAM) trips lead by George Paine. I include some notes that I made when I went to the place, and I have categorized the places by the primary fish that I have caught there.

There should be more than enough places in this Appendix to get you started; however, there are much better books on the subject than this one. For example, there is Harry Murray's "TROUT FISHING IN THE SHENANDOAH NATIONAL PARK". In it he gives you the driving routes and some information about the parking available. I highly recommend that you get a book like this so you don't arrive in the area where you want to fish and not know where to turn off the main drag and/or where to safely park. Actually, parking is the sticky point. You usually can't just park off the road, but rather each fishing spot has its own unique situation for parking.

An example of what I mean is the parking for fishing the Hughes River. There are only three parking spots near where I like to fish so I get there early. You can walk up the road to more spots, but that means more walking.

Note that all directions below are relative to starting from the Vienna, Virginia area.

15.1 Mainly Sunfish

Manassas Ponds: There are several ponds on the Manassas Battlefield National Park. Since the ponds are so close to my house, I fish there a lot. I have caught many bluegill and a few smallmouth bass at the ponds. I do all of my pond fishing from shore, but there are times when I need to cross a creek and wished that I had some hip waders, or at least some waterproof boots.

15 APPENDIX A

The people at the Park Headquarters can point you to where the various ponds are located. Be aware, however, that you have to have a valid Virginia fishing license in addition to the National Park permit. I have been checked twice. In my case, I have a lifetime Virginia license (with a trout stamp) and a Golden Age Passport for the National Parks, so I am all set any time that I want to fish. By the way, this allows me to fish the National Parks and Forests as well.

I have also caught sunfish in the North Fork of the Shenandoah River, Passage Creek and some mountain streams (see below for more information on those places).

15.2 Mainly Stocked Rainbow Trout

Passage Creek: This is a nice place to fish. It has good parking and is stocked in the fall. On October 21, 2005 Passage Creek had just been stocked and so the fishing was excellent for big rainbows. I actually quit early because it was too easy. I went back the next week and they were much more selective, but still quite catchable.

The place where I fish Passage Creek is near the Fish Hatchery off Route 678 (Fort Valley Road). To get to it, take Interstate 66 to Front Royal and take the Route 522/340 exit going towards Front Royal. Turn right onto Route 55, which goes to Strasburg. Drive down the road until you see a cemetery on the left. Turn left onto Route 678. Follow the road for about a mile and then turn left where you see the sign to the Fish Hatchery. By the way, if you continue on up Route 678 you come to the George Washington (GW) National Park where there are a lot of places to fish Passage Creek (Have your permit for the National Parks, however).

On December 1, 2006, the creek was raging at the usual place that I visit, near the hatchery, so I walked up to a part of the creek that was quieter. It was near where Fort Valley Road first meets the creek near the entrance into the GW National Forest. I caught two nice size rainbows (about 14 inches). Actually this trip was a test for me. I wanted to see where my air temperature limit was. I must admit that I am a fair weather fisherman, so if it is too uncomfortable, then I am not going fishing. On this day the water temperature was 42 degrees and the air temp about 46 degrees. In addition, there was no sun. This is too cold for me!

Big Stoney Creek: I have never fished there, but I gather it is like Passage Creek in that they stock it in the fall. There are several places to park along the way from Interstate 66 on Route 675 (Stoney Creek Road) to Columbia Furnace. Per the folks at Murray's Fly Shop in Edinburg, it is okay to park anywhere along the creek from the Furnace to Interstate 66, as long as it is not posted otherwise.

15.3 Mainly Brook Trout

Upper Rapidan River: From Interstate 66 south, exit at Route 29 south. Drive south on Route 29 past Warrenton and continue towards to Culpeper. Don't go into Culpeper, but rather take the bypass on Route 29 out around it. Take a right onto Route 609 until it dead-ends into Route 231. Turn right on Route 231 and follow it to the town of Banco. Turn left onto Route 670, going to Criglersville. A little past Criglersville, turn left onto Route 649 (Quaker Run) up to the forest. Take the fire road to the Upper Rapidan. There is parking and fishing all along river. This is where the Murray's Mountain Trout School went after the lectures. It's great fishing, but the fire road can be very rutted, so an SUV or truck is best. I did make it two times, however, in my 1996 Dodge Avenger, so it can be done if you really want to. [Since writing the above, the fire road has been serviced and it is a lot easier to use. It will deteriorate of course, but should be okay for awhile.]

On April 11, 2005 when we went to the Upper Rapidan during the trout school, the water temperature was 46 degrees. I caught ten brookies on Mr. Rapidan #14 and #16 dry flies. The air temperature was about 65 to 70 degrees, so it was really nice to be outside. The next day, I caught twelve brookies on #14 Bead Head Nymph. On this day, it was overcast and colder, so it was not as nice, but catching the brookies made up for it.

Lower Piney River: Take Route 211 south out of Warrenton to just above Sperryville. Route 522 comes into Route 211 at Massies Corner. Continue on Route 211/522 south. Turn right onto Route 612 (Old Hollow Road). Be careful to bear right at all times since Route 612 turns left where Route 600 intersects it, and it looks like it is a different road.

Follow Route 600 until you arrive at a brick walled estate on your right. Route 653 goes off to the left over the Lower Piney. There are barely two parking spots just beyond the bridge. See the "My First Brookie" chapter for more on my first trip to the Lower Piney. It tells you how to get there and the crazy parking situation.

I am going to tell you about one of my later trips when I knew a little more about what I was doing. The water temperature was 52 degrees and the day was sunny. I caught several brookies and even what looked to be some small largemouth bass!

I used a Light Cahill to start. I wasn't "matching the hatch," I just put it on blindly because it looked like something that the fish would want. Who knows what was hatching on that day? I caught a seven inch brookie on it; then I had a lot of misses. I figured that they were small brookies, so I switched to a #16 Sulphur. I caught three more. Later I found a pool where I could see lots of fish; however, there were no takers on top. I switched to a nymph. I had no luck using just the nymph with no weight on it, so I put a split shot six inches above it to get it down faster. This did the trick and I caught four fish. The take-away lesson is to get the nymph down to the bottom!!!

15 APPENDIX A

Hughes River: Go to Sperryville on Route 211 out of Warrenton. Route 522 comes into Route 211 at Massies Corner. Follow Route 522 out of Sperryville going south (Route 211 goes north up to Skyline Drive. Don't go that way unless you want to fish the Blue Ridge streams from up top!). Follow Route 522 for a little bit and then turn right onto Route 231 going south. Follow it until you cross the Hughes. Turn right and follow the road until almost where it ends. The road follows the Hughes up to a very large parking lot for Old Rag Mountain, which is on your left. You want to go a little farther up the road. I am not going to give you route numbers in this case as there are several involved. Just follow the road, keeping the Hughes on your right.

I saw many places to pull off just after turning onto the road, and several fishermen on the river, so it must be okay to do this. There were no signs prohibiting it that I saw, except in a few places. Most of the fishermen were spincasters, but I did see one fly-fisherman. I tried it one other time and didn't have any luck. On that outing some spincasters on the bank who could see down to the river said that they saw some large rainbows that had been stocked recently. I was wading and couldn't see them. I probably spooked them. I think that I could do better now.

The place where I park to fish the Hughes is just past the large Old Rag Mountain parking lot. There is about a three car parking place right at Nicholson Hollow Trail where you can walk into the Park. There is also a large parking lot up further the road from the three car parking spot.

To the left of the three car parking area (facing it from the road), you will see a stone post that says "Nicholson Hollow Trail." Go down the road (which is actually the driveway for a private residence) to the driveway gate and you will see a sign for the Nicholson Hollow Trail sign pointing off to the right. It says that the park is 1/2 mile up the trail and that the land up to that point is private. Go down the trail, cross Brokenback Run via some rocks in the Run, continue up a little bit and then cross the Hughes by means of some more rocks. Follow the trail until you get to the Shenandoah National Park sign. The Hughes is bigger past this point.

I have fished the Hughes many times with mixed success. One time the water temperature was 56 degrees and I caught two brookies and another fish with a big mouth and silver scales (Sorry, but I'm still a newbie so I can't identify a lot of fish on sight). A guy I asked thought that it was a rock fish. By the way, that day I got there at 8 AM and there were two cars before me. Luckily there was an open spot.

On another day, when I was feeling pretty good about catching three brookies, I met a guy who said that he had gotten there at 6:30 AM and had caught 15 fish in the first hour or so, plus 40 fish after that (40 fish? What were they doing, jumping onto the fly?). He said that he had used a parachute ADAMS. I caught ten good brookies a week later on a parachute

ADAMS, so I guess he was right on the fly, and was obviously a lot better fisherman than I was/am, or maybe he was stretching the truth a little bit.

Brokenback Run: Follow the directions to the Hughes River to get to this water. Brokenback Run enters the Hughes near the three car parking spot that I use for the Hughes. The day that I fished the Run, the water temperature was 48 degrees. I caught seven brookies, two on a Prince Nymph without a split shot (no bites with split shot). I also caught five really small fish on a Light Cahill, which matched what I saw on the stream in color and size. I didn't know what the heck was hatching. Brokenback Run takes a lot of effort since it has a lot of rocks and you have to do a lot of climbing. Be careful not to violate any property rights. It's best to park in the larger lot beyond the three car one and walk down to Brokenback Run where you know for sure that you are in the Park.

Hazel River: Go to Sperryville on Route 522/211 out of Warrenton (see the directions to the Hughes above). Follow Route 522 out of Sperryville, going south (Route 211 goes north up to Skyline Drive.). Follow Route 522 for a little bit and then turn right onto Route 231 going south. Follow it for about ten minutes until you see a sign for Route 681 (Rolling Road). This will be just <u>before</u> you cross the Hazel. Go to the narrow bridge. The road splits here. Take the right fork that follows the river. Park anywhere along river.

The one day that I went the water temperature was 68 degrees. The good news is that it is closer than the Hughes River; the bad news is that it doesn't have deep pools, has lots of canopy and very small fish. I won't go back. I caught about seven redside dace (minnows) on a small parachute ant. I could have caught more, but I got tired of the small fish.

By the way, I have followed the river up quite a ways, but didn't see anything better than what I had fished. There may be some places, however, because one of the locals that I meet when I fish the Hughes told me that he fishes there, and I can't believe that he would be satisfied with the small fish that I caught. Maybe if I went really far up, but I haven't tried, and don't intend to.

White Oak Canyon: Drive south on Route 29 (Bypass) to Culpeper (see the directions to the Upper Rapidan above). Continue on Route 29 out of Culpeper. Take a right on Route 609 until it dead-ends into Route 231. Turn right on Route 231 and follow it to Banco. Turn left onto Route 670 going to Criglersville. Take a right onto Route 600 and you will see signs to the parking lot at White Oak Canyon. It is right off Route 600. It is a really popular hiking spot and I have seen a lot of families there. It is two hours from Vienna to the White Oak Canyon parking lot, and one hour from Warrenton.

One day when I fished the canyon, the water temperature was 46 degrees. It was mostly sunny with an air temperature of about 65 degrees - delightful. There wasn't a lot of leaf cover yet. I fished the lower part of White Oak Canyon and caught four brookies on a #14

Bead Head Nymph. There were lots of pools spoiled due to my hooking twigs, etc. I had no luck fishing with the Mr. Rapidan dry fly for an hour, which is why I switched to the nymph. Another reason that I switched to the nymph was because I did not see any rises. Maybe this is because the water was a little high and running fast.

Little Stoney Creek in the George Washington National Forest: Take Interstate 66 west to Interstate 81 south to Woodstock. Go west on Route 42 to Columbia Furnace. Immediately after you cross the "Big" Stoney River, turn right. It will be a 180 degree turn, so be careful! You will go across a one-lane bridge over the Stoney. Make an immediate left onto Route 675 and continue down until you see Route 608. Turn right onto Route 608. Continue on for awhile and be on the lookout for a fireroad that enters from the left. It is a clear intersection, but not clearly marked. The road is Fireroad 92.

While driving on Fireroad 92, you will pass a very large dirt parking lot on the left, but continue on. A little farther up the road you will cross the Little Stoney, but probably won't recognize that you have done so because the creek goes through a large corrugated metal pipe under the road. However, immediately after you cross the creek, there will be a clearly marked parking lot off to the left. It has room for about eight cars and a big park information board so you should know that you are in the right place.

By the way, if you miss the turnoff on Route 608, you can continue on Route 675 until the Fireroad 92 meets it. Here it comes in from the right, so turn right onto it and go to the parking lot, which will now be on your right.

Rose River: Drive south on Route 29 (Bypass) to Culpeper (see the directions above for the Upper Rapidan for a little more detail if you need it). Continue on Route 29 out of Culpeper. Take a right on Route 609 until it dead-ends into Route 231. Turn right on Route 231 and follow it to Banco. Turn left onto Route 670 going to Criglersville. You will go past Graves Mountain Lodge, which will be on your left. Continue all the way to the end of the road (it is 1.7 miles of gravel road at the very end). There is fairly good parking there, park as near to the end of the road as possible because, apparently, some of the locals do not like more than about 3 cars parking from the end of the road. Access to the Park is very near and the Rose River is right there.

Our FWAM group fished the Rose early in December 2004. No one had much luck. Those that did used an elk hair caddis after it warmed up (about 2:30 PM) and nymphs. I didn't catch anything. I have gone back since and caught four good size brookies. You can go straight down to the river after you enter the Park or walk up a bit. It's your choice. Walking has the advantage of not following someone else. There is a bridge a ways up on the Park trail where there are some nice pools.

15.4 Mainly Smallmouth Bass (near Washington, D. C.)

Point of Rocks on the Potomac River: I haven't fished here a lot, but did catch a bluegill one day. Thank goodness for bluegills. Both of the times that I have gone it has been high, muddy and flowing too fast. It was about waist high where I fished near the first bridge support. Per the River Gauge on the Internet, the river was at 4.7 feet and was at 16% of flood flow. I would say it needed to be at about 3 feet and 5% of flood flow for good fishing.

Riverbend Park on the Potomac River: It is off Georgetown Pike going from the Capitol Beltway (Interstate 495) towards Sterling, Virginia. Watch for signs to the park off to the right. You are not encouraged to wade in the river, but apparently they either can't legally stop you or don't enforce it if they can. I have been told by some individuals that they fish there regularly, so I don't know what the rules are. I would check before doing any wading to see what the latest thinking is.

I have only fished at Riverbend once, and that was from the shore, which is not the way to go. If you have a boat, it is a good place to launch it. When I was spincasting, my wife and I would rent a boat and fish the Potomac mainly for smallmouth bass. They stopped renting boats a while back, which is a big reason why I gave up fishing until recently. They are supposed to start renting again according to a person in the Information Lodge. (Since I have my own pontoon boat now, I fish Riverbend quite a bit. As I said previously, I won't talk about my pontoon boat experience since I believe that it is beyond the scope of this book.)

Fletcher's Boat House for the Potomac River: See the "Shad Fiasco and Redemption" chapter for this fishing place. I have included this reference to it here for completeness.

Violette's Lock for the Potomac River: My wife and I checked out Violette's Lock since it was pointed out to me on one of the times that I went to The Angler's Lie Flyshop. It is very good from an access and parking standpoint. The parking is close to the river and there are Portajohns. It is 12 miles from the Beltway. You take River Road from the Beltway through the town of Potomac. It is seven miles beyond Swain's Lock which is well marked. Continue on and take the first left after Manor Stone Drive on a right curve. Be careful because it is not well marked in this direction. If you have gone to where River Road has a stop sign, then you have gone too far.

I have fished Violette's Lock only once and didn't have much luck. It looked fishable, but a little high. The water temperature was more than 78 degrees (the reading was off my thermometer). The gauge at Little Falls read 3.15 feet and 3690 cfs (2% of flood flow). It was not bad wading, but I didn't catch any bass. I caught three bluegills (one was nine inches). I found that it was too hard to get out to the river and when you do, you don't know where the fish are since the river is so wide. I think that a boat would be an advantage here.

Goose Creek near Leesburg -- It is just off of Rte 7: I really had a lot of hope for this spot since it is so close to my house, but it didn't pan out. I fished it a couple of times. One time I left the house at 5:46AM and arrived in the parking lot at 6:24AM for a trip total of 38 minutes. It is 28 miles from my house in Vienna to the parking lot. The creek was quite fishable, but the water was discolored. The gauge at Little Falls read 211 cfs and 1.9 feet. I caught two sunfish and one smallie.

The problem with Goose Creek that I can see is that since the creek gets so low at times there is no way there can be a resident population of fish unless they come up from the Potomac. On my second visit, however, I did catch a very nice size smallie, but that was the only fish.

I have seen other people coming back from the Potomac direction after fishing, so others apparently seem to think that it is worth while. However I won't be going back.

15.5 Mainly Smallmouth Bass (Front Royal, Woodstock, etc.)

North Fork of the Shenandoah River near Woodstock: [Be aware that as of this entry date of February 6, 2007, there have been pollution problems with the North Fork and South Fork of the Shenandoah River. You might want to check with Murray's Fly Shop for what the current situation is before traveling any great distance to fish them.] Take Interstate 66 to Interstate 81 to Woodstock, Virginia. I have fished several places along the North Fork in this area, for example, Chapman's Landing. See the Potomac Appalachian Trail Club maps for other access points in the Woodstock area.

This used to be my favorite river for smallies until the recent revelations about fish kills and frankenfish (I caught one smallie that was pink and had several sore-like marks on its body). When I was fishing the North Fork, I usually checked the Strasburg gauge online to see what the river level was and its flow rate before going. I have checked it many times after I have gone fishing to correlate what the gauge said with what I saw. I have found that it is the water flow rate that is most important since you can always find shallower spots to fish. A high flow rate, however, is tough to wade in.

For example, on October 4, 2004 I went fishing, and it was too high and too fast. The Strasburg gauge read 3.6 feet and 5% of flood flow. On October 8, 2004, I tried my spot and it was still too fast. The Strasburg gauge read 2.77 feet and 3% of flood flow. I estimate that it would have to be 1.5 feet and no more than 1% of flood flow to get the water where I have fished in the Woodstock -Edinburg area to be what I would like it to be. By the way, there is another reason that the flow rate is important, namely, because the river is too dangerous to cross when the flow rate is too high, you can't get to the shaded side of it, thereby eliminating a lot of potential targets. The following table gives my personal "wade-ability estimate" given the Strasburg gauge reading at the time.

Table 15-1 Strasburg River Gauge Reading Relative to Wade-ability

Here are the gauge readings together with what I found for wading when I went to the North Fork of the Shenandoah River at access points near Woodstock, Virginia.

- Gauge Reading: 3.6 feet and 5% of flood flow (1335 cubic feet per second, cfs). It was **not** wadeable.
- Gauge Reading: 2.77 feet and 3% of flood flow (801 cfs). It was **not** wadeable.
- Gauge Reading: 2.18 feet and 1% of flood flow (267 cfs). It was **wadeable**, but a little high and fast (I caught 23 fish on it, however).
- Gauge Reading: 2.12 feet and 240 cfs. **Perfect for wading !!!** (I caught over 30 fish including a 14 inch fallfish.)

By the way, there is no access at Strasburg that I know of (I drove down Route 11 from Strasburg to Woodstock one time to check this out); even if you could, there are tall trees on both sides of the river near Strasburg.

Chapman's Landing on the North Fork of Shenandoah River: Take Interstate 66 west to Interstate 81 south. Get off on Route 42 east. Follow Route 42 until it intersects Route 11. Turn right and follow Route 11 south to just above Edinburg.

Chapman's Landing is a left turn off Route 11 just after you cross a bridge. You will see a sign for "The Inn at Narrow Passage". After turning left follow the road past the entrance to the Inn, which is on your right, and park in the lot on your left prior to the one-lane car bridge. You can fish anywhere along the lot or wade upstream and downstream.

If you go just beyond the pedestrian bridge upstream, which you can see from the parking lot, the river is a lot like my favorite North Fork spot farther up the river. It is deep in the channel and has a lot of rocks on the bottom. Beyond this point the river is not as deep. One of the days that I was there, the river was low, but there was still plenty of water for good fishing (bluegills, smallies, fallfish). The Strasburg gauge showed 1.82 feet and 128 cfs. I caught over ten fish, albeit not large ones. I saw several monster fallfish, but they wouldn't take anything that I threw at them. I guess they were not hungry.

Covered Bridge at Mt. Jackson for the North Fork of Shenandoah River: A nice lady who works at Murray's Fly Shop told me about this location when the river near there was too high. Take Interstate 66 west to Interstate 81 south. Get off on Route 263 east at Mount Jackson. Go to Route 11. Turn right onto Route 11. Follow it until it crosses the North

Fork. Go a little farther and you will see a sign on the right for the covered bridge. Turn right onto Wissler Road (It is spelled "Wisler Road" on another map). Go up to the covered bridge and park on the left.

This is a good place to fish if the river at Chapman's Landing and other places near Woodstock or Edinburg are flowing too fast. There is less water because it is above a major stream that enters the North Fork. One time when I went there it was still running high; however, it was much better than the accesses at Edinburg or Woodstock. It has plenty of parking and is easy to get to the river. I suggest wading upstream or downstream from the bridge to get away from people.

The second time that I went to Mt. Jackson, the Strasburg gauge read 369 cfs and 2.4 feet, so going to Woodstock was out of the question. At Mt. Jackson, however, it was easily wadeable and I caught 18 smallies within site of the bridge. I went upstream and caught a big one in the rapids. There is also a nice pool very near the bridge on the opposite side.

Bentonville for the South Fork of the Shenandoah River: This is a place that is really popular with spincasters as there is a lot of shore access, and you can put in boats. There is also a big parking lot very near the river. I have never fished it, however, because several times when I have gone there, the river was too high and flowing too fast or otherwise was not wadeable. To get to it, take Interstate 66 west. Get off at Route 638 south at Linden. Turn right onto Route 55 and follow it until it dead ends into Route 340 south. Follow Route 340 south out of Front Royal to Bentonville. You will see signs to the one-lane bridge. There is an outfitter there. To get to the parking lot you have to go across the one-lane bridge. The lot is on your right.

Andrew Guest State Park for the South Fork of the Shenandoah River: I have only fished it once when I was very, very new to fly-fishing. I didn't catch anything, but that means nothing. I will try it again now that I know a little more about what I am doing. There is a nominal entrance fee to get into the park. It has some nice facilities and good parking. The river is quite nice to fish there. To get to it follow my directions for Bentonville above, but just a little bit after you leave Front Royal you will see an entrance to Skyline Drive on the left. Go a bit farther down Route 340 going south and you will see a sign for the Andrew Guest State Park. It will be on your right.

15.6 Mainly Smallmouth Bass (Near Culpeper, VA)

Kelly's Ford: This is my favorite spot for smallmouth bass now, both because of the Shenandoah River pollution and it is a half an hour closer to my house. I go towards Culpeper, past Warrenton on its bypass road, and follow Route 29/15 (Routes 29 and 15 merge for a while) until you see the sign to Kelly's Ford Inn. This is Kelley's Ford Road. Turn left off of Route 29/15 and immediately cross some railroad tracks. After crossing the tracks, turn left and follow the road to the bridge over the Rappahannock River. There is good parking on either side of the bridge. The first lot has a boat launch.

I have fished both upstream and downstream from the bridge with a lot of success. My go-to fly for this river is a black flash Wooly Bugger with a bead head. I have also caught smallies on blue or white poppers, crayfish and strymphs. When they are biting, pretty much anything catches fish. I have been skunked, however, but this was late in the season, so it probably wasn't me. When I say skunked, I mean for smallies. There are lots of bluegills to be had, and some are nice sized ones.

Here is some further information about Kelley's Ford that I can pass on to you as the result of some of my outings. I had lots of luck on June 7, 2006 with a Shenandoah Blue Popper and the black flash bead head Wooly Bugger. By the way, I am telling you the date so that you know that it was in the spring when the smallmouth bass are starting to bite and are easy to catch, as opposed to my superior angling skills. Anyway, I caught about 20 fish, including a 13" smallmouth, some good size fallfish and two 9" pumpkinseeds. I was fishing upstream from the bridge where there are lots of rocks. The wading was great! The Remington gauge read 200 cfs and 3.2 feet. My guess is that it would be good until about 3.75 feet. The gauge at Fredricksburg read 409 cfs and 2.3 feet. Of course, the Rappahannock and the Lower Rapidan have merged by then, so it would naturally read higher.

On another trip in June, I saw a really big fish with a red stripe on its side jump in front of me. I later saw it swimming. I'd guess that it was around 25" long. It would not take anything that I threw, however. It didn't get that big by being dumb, I guess.

On September 7, 2006, I went downstream from the bridge. It is very similar in structure to the North Fork of the Shenandoah where I used to fish. It has a lot of rocks and tall trees on either side for shade. I caught about five fish on a black flash Wooly Bugger, including a 13" fall fish, 7" and 9" smallies and a 7" sunfish. I also got hits on a popper too, but they were too small to be caught on the size fly that I was presenting to them at the time. The river was borderline, too high and fast to fish. The Remington gauge read 434 cfs and 3.8 feet. I think that ideal fishing would be a gauge reading of 100 to 200 cfs and 3 feet.

Eleys Ford: There may be shorter ways to get to Eleys Ford, but one way is to follow Route 3 south and east just below Culpeper until you get to the town of Lignum. Turn left onto Revercomb Road. Follow it until you see Eleys Ford Road going off to the right. Follow it until you get to the bridge over the Lower Rapidan. Coming from that direction, the exit to the boat ramp is on your left just over the bridge and not very visible, so go slowly as you cross the bridge.

15 APPENDIX A

I have only fished Eleys Ford once, but had great luck. It was on June 9, 2006, and the Lower Rapidan gauge near Culpeper was 150 cfs and 0.88 feet. The Lower Rapidan at Eleys Ford has a very sandy bottom at the boat launch. There wasn't much for rocks until I went downstream around the bend in the river. There is a really deep pool there. I had my best success fishing the bank on the boat launch side (east side) of the Lower Rapidan while going down to this pool. The east side of the Lower Rapidan is deeper than the other bank and was shadier at the time that I was fishing. I used a Shenandoah Blue Popper, a <u>black</u> flash bead head Wooly Bugger and a Crayfish. I saw refusals on an <u>olive</u> flash Wooly Bugger!

Here is a lesson that I learned for the popper when I fished Eleys Ford. I saw the fish come up under the popper, look at it for a good half a minute, and then hit it. So when using a popper, try casting it and letting it sit for a good while. Then you can move it and let it sit again. When I was "swimming" the popper, it spooked the fish. I have had luck swimming poppers in other situations, however, so try both ways.

16 Appendix B
My Flybox Contents

I have tried several flyboxes up to this point. The one that I like for my bass flies (the bigger ones) is the Scientific Anglers "System" flybox, whereas the one that I use for the trout flies is the Orvis ribbed flybox. The foam on the bass box (that's what I call it) is easier to deal with in taking the flies in and out. It is too coarse for the smaller flies, however.

It is your choice as to picking a ribbed or a flat foam inside of the flybox itself. I like the ribbed one since it is easier to take the flies in and out of it. Both of my boxes have the ribbed inside.

I haven't had any problems with my bass box, however, my trout box has the problem of the foam not holding a fly if the point is put into a hole that has been made by a previous fly hook point. I may replace this one later, but it does the job for now.

I have included a picture of my flybox contents (one for trout and the other for bass and shad) as of March 24, 2005. It hasn't changed much since then. I only include it to give you some idea of what I use. As you can see in the figure below, I don't have a lot, but it has seemed to work for me so far. It also illustrates that you don't need every fly ever invented to have fun fly-fishing.

16 APPENDIX B

Trout Flybox Contents (March 24, 2005)

Left Side
Adams   Sulphurs
Royal Coachman   Royal Wulff
Fly Imitations
Mr. Rapidan Dry Flies
Dark Cahill   Light Cahill
Caddis
No Name Damsel Terrestrials

Right Side
Hare's Ear Nymphs
Prince Nymph   Mr. Rapidan Emergers
Red Squirrel Nymph
Black Nose Dace   Mickey Finn
Wooly Bugger   Strymph

Figure 16-1 Trout Flybox Contents

Bass/Shad Flybox Contents (March 24, 2005)

Left Side
Strymphs, Leadeyed Hellgramites, Wooly Buggers, Zonkers

Right Side
Shad Darts
Mickey Fins, Sneaky Petes
Lefty's Deceivers
Wooly Buggers, Leadeyed Hellgramites, Strymphs,

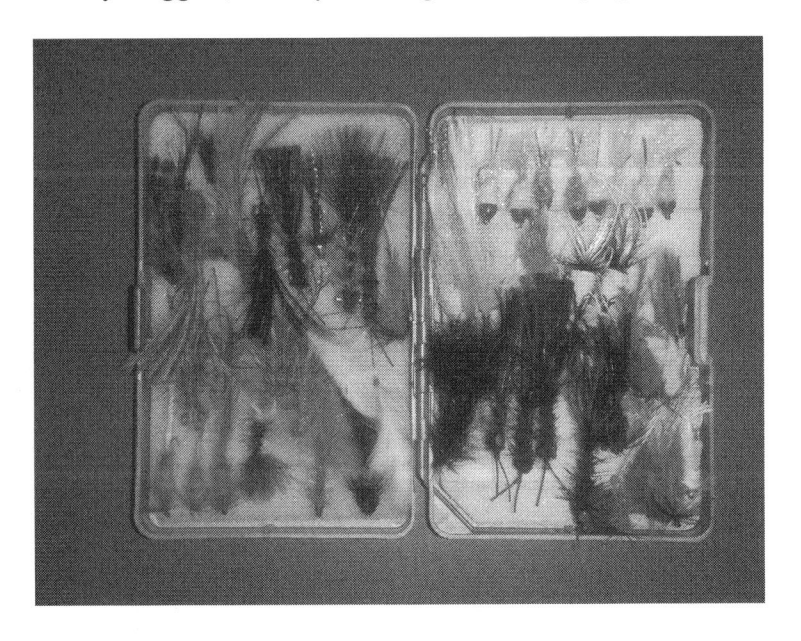

Figure 16-2 Bass/Shad Flybox Contents

17 Appendix C
ROSS Cimarron 3 Reel Setup

In the original setup from The Angler's Lie, Newell Steele put on 468 feet of 20# backing along with the 88.5 feet of 7 weight fly line.

For the sinking line, I put on 400 feet of backing for the 105 feet of sinking line. I could have used more backing (I would guess about 70 feet), but it is okay the way it is. The instructions below call for about 3/16 inch from the wound line to the edge of the spool. Newell's rigging resulted in 4/16 inch. I got 6/16 inch (close enough I think, but I will see how it casts, etc.). I can always add backing later. [Note: Since writing this I have used the sinking line for shad and it casts just fine.]

By the way, when I setup my spare reel with the sinking line, I measured everything!!! I laid out a tape measure from the utility room to the main basement room (about 30 feet). I then used 2 dowels to wrap backing and fly line around them until I got the measurements that I needed. I then wound the backing and line onto the reel using the vise to secure the reel. I believe in trust, but verify.

Table 17-1 ROSS Cimarron 3 Specifications

Width (spool): 80 inches
Diameter: 3.5 inches
Weight: 5.0 oz.
Line Weights: 6 to 8 Wt.
Capacity: WF6 (Weight Forward, 6 Weight) fly line with 160 yards of 20# backing

Line capacities are based on floating fly lines and 20# backing. The fly line capacities will vary according to the specific length and diameters of the line manufactures' products.

18 Appendix D
After-Season Fishing Gear Cleanup

There are many places that tell you how to clean up your gear in preparation for the spring fishing season. This appendix is going to tell you what I personally did and how I did it. Note that I do not fish in salt water, so cleanup would be different for that. The process below is for fresh water fishing.

Fly line
- First I cleaned and preserved my fly line. By the way, I rinse it with clean water after every few fishing outings to get the grime off of it. After several outings I put some fly line dressing on it after I wash, rinse and dry it. Periodically, I run my finger along the fly line. If I feel a roughness, then it is getting bad.
- I did one fly line at a time. (Doing more than one can get really confusing unless you have enough space to separate them.)
- I used a mild dish water detergent (IVORY cake soap is recommended in a lot of books) to wash the line in a large shallow plastic pan in the basement sink.
- I took the pan out of the sink and rinsed the line in the sink.
- I dried the line with a towel.
- I pulled out the line and laid it on the floor of our longest room, which happens to be in the basement. I used paint cloths to protect the rug.
- I put the reel on a finishing nail that I nailed into the wood shelves on one side of the room, and pulled the line out to a hutch in the other side of the room.
- I used a piece of cloth and applied the fly line dressing.
- I used a clean cloth and removed the excess dressing.
- I put more Pliobond on <u>the loop</u> at the end of the fly line to make it run through the guides better. This step may or may not be needed, depending on the condition of the loop.

Reels
I have three reels, the ROSS reel for my 7 weight line, the Hardy reel for my 3 weight line, and the Orvis reel for my 5 weight line. I simply followed the cleaning directions for each of them. After all, the manufacturers know their reel best and what it takes to keep it in good working order.

All Rods

I simply washed the rods with dishwater detergent including the cork handles and let them dry for several days. I checked the guides with a nylon stocking to see if they had any burrs. They didn't.

Waders

I used the "inflation" method for testing the integrity of the waders. I attached my shop vacuum to the open part of the waders and used a bungee cord to make a tight connection. I then turned on the vacuum, <u>making sure that I didn't build up too much pressure on the waders</u>.

With the waders expanded and under some pressure on the inside, I took some soapy water and brushed it all over the waders. As I was doing it, I looked for leaks, which would have shown themselves by producing bubbles. As it turns out the waders did not leak. I didn't think that I had a problem because I have been dry after a fishing trip.

Since my waders have multiple layers, I wondered if there could be a leak in an inner layer and not show up in the test, so I ask the salesman at Orvis who sold me the waders. **He said that basically you could sit in a tub with them on, and if you didn't feel wet then you were okay. I like that advice!**

A nice thing about my waders is that the place where they get the most wear and/or where they would be subject to punctures is reinforced. So unless I get tangled in a stickerbush and rip myself away, I should not have any leaks for an awful long time. You get what you pay for.

19 Appendix E
Tam and I

One of the things that drew me to fly-fishing was that it reminded me of the days when my half Airedale, half terrier dog Tammy (shown below) and I would go out to explore the woods and streams near our house. We found crayfish and minnows and were in our own world. Many days I never saw another person for several hours, and it was great!

When I am walking in the Shenandoah Mountains or standing in a river, I am brought back to my youth. I actually have the same feeling that I had back then. For this reason I am including a poem that I wrote awhile ago about my dog and those days. I hope that you enjoy it.

Figure 19-1 My Dog Tam

19 APPENDIX E

Tam and I

So far away those days it seems,
When as a boy we roamed the hills.
Tam and I would cross the streams,
And hoped and prayed there'd be no spills.

A bright new day would never end,
Or so it was in times gone past.
Tam and I would search the glen.
Oh how I wished those days did last.

But lo, the times speed by.
I cannot make them stay.
Tam is gone, for all things die.
We can no longer play.

No more the woods and o'er the field
Romping to and fro.
Tam and I have had to yield.
We've had to let life go.

I am so very grateful for
That dog with wagging tongue.
And all those precious days of yore
When Tam and I were young.

David E. Cartier
April 12, 2000

Index

B
Boots 10, 18, 19, 23, 38

C
Casting 11, 31, 39, 67, 85

D
DeLORME 5, 71, 74

F
Fish
    Bluegill 6, 12, 13, 22, 25, 26, 53, 74, 80, 82
    Brook Trout 12, 16, 24, 36-38, 71
    Rainbow Trout 12, 37, 75
    Shad 13, 40, 43-45, 55, 68, 80
    Smallmouth Bass 26, 80, 81, 83
    Trout 29, 30, 35, 36, 38, 39, 71
Fish With A Member (FWAM) Trip 4, 16, 22, 74, 79
Flies
    Streamers 11, 12, 25, 26, 27, 29, 30, 39, 69

K
Knots 5, 14, 41, 60, 62, 63
    Duncan Loop (aka Uni-knot) 14, 63
    Uni-knot (aka Duncan Loop) 63, 64, 65

L
L. L. Bean Fly Shop 4, 7, 8, 9, 11, 18, 33, 51, 52, 68, 73
Leaders 5, 13-15, 22, 30, 31, 41, 42, 58, 59
Leisenring Lift For Nymphing 33, 34, 49

M
Manassas, VA 6, 74
Murray, Harry 12, 25, 28, 32, 56, 74
Murray, Jeff 32

N
Neoprene Wader Material 10
Nymphing Technique 28, 29, 34, 47
Nymphs 15, 21, 24, 28-30, 33, 35, 39, 72, 76, 78, 79, 87

94

INDEX

O
Orvis Fly Shop 4, 5, 8, 10, 12, 18, 73, 86, 90, 91

P
pH of Water...34, 35, 69, 71, 72

R
Reels...5, 12, 28, 41, 42, 44, 55, 58, 60, 90
Rivers
    Potomac..4, 13, 42, 71, 72, 74, 80, 81
    Shenandoah 2, 7, 10, 16, 23, 24, 25, 32, 34, 74, 77, 81, 82, 83
    Shenandoah North Fork 16, 25, 26, 75, 81, 82
Rods 5, 12-14, 25, 28, 44, 55, 57, 58, 66-68
    3 Weight Line 5, 12, 25, 56, 60, 90
    5 Weight Line 5, 12, 25, 68, 90
    7 Weight Line 5, 12, 13, 44, 60, 68, 89, 90

S
Simms Fishing Gear...8, 10
Sinking
    Sinking Lines 40-42, 44-46, 55, 89
    Sinking Tips 41
Steele, Newell 40, 89

T
Tippets... 5, 13-15, 21, 29, 35, 36, 39, 44, 55, 59, 69
Trout Unlimited Organization..1, 3, 16, 18, 22, 71, 73

V
Vests...7, 8, 59, 68
Vises..52, 53

W
Waders 10, 18, 19, 23, 74, 91
    Gortex 10
Wading Sticks 11, 20, 70

Z
ZEBCO Fishing Outfits 6, 17